Brain Worms

Brain Worms

How Right-Wing Propaganda Destroys
Reason, Conscience, and Democracy

AG PRESS

Morgantown

© 2021 Adam Glenn.

Published in 2021 by A.G. Press

ISBN-13: 978-0-578-99632-5

Cover design by Adam Glenn.

Library of Congress Cataloging-in-Publication data is available.

10 9 8 7 6 5 4 3 2 1

Contents

	Introduction	1
1	Conservatism	12
2	Classical Liberalism	42
3	Constitutionalism	61
4	Capitalism	81
5	Economics 101	110
6	Personal Responsibility	138
7	The Party of Lincoln	154
8	The PC Thought Police	180
	Notes	198

For Sarah, Norah, and Emily

Introduction

The American right is running humanity off a cliff. Climate change is accelerating, threatening to make the world unlivable for future generations. Social and economic inequality continue to worsen, preventing millions of people from living up to their potential. We're lucky we haven't blown ourselves up yet in a nuclear war—the possibility of which is now greater than ever. Our political institutions are becoming brittle, preventing us from governing ourselves in accordance with our goals. These problems persist despite readily available solutions—a Green New Deal, cooperating with other nations to reduce the proliferation of nuclear weapons, a stronger social safety net, drastically raising taxes on the rich, expanding voting rights, removing impediments to governance (such as the Senate filibuster), and so on—all of which enjoy widespread public support.

Why, then, do the problems facing America persist? Because the right has driven half the country insane. They've spent decades inundating us with propaganda, which has destroyed much of our capacity to consider, let alone implement readily-available solutions. The right's propaganda prevents society from being able to talk rationally about important social problems, erodes empathy for those who are disadvantaged by our current economic and political system, promotes a cult of selfishness, and is meant to undermine democracy at every turn.

What's the right's goal? To protect power and privilege. The right knows that any solution to society's problems requires redistributing wealth and power away from America's corporate elite and into the hands of the people. To combat climate change, we have to take power away from the fossil fuel industry. To minimize the possibility of nuclear war, we have to take power away from the military-industrial complex. To reduce social and economic inequality, we have to take power away from corporations and the rich. Doing these things requires stronger regulation, higher taxes, more social spending, and reforms that make our political system more democratic. The right doesn't like this idea. Following through on these reforms would diminish the One Percent's grip on our political and economic system. The right must therefore trick large swaths of the population into believing what's good for corporate America and the rich—lower taxes, fewer regulations, "smaller" government—is what's good for everyone.

I wrote this book to shed light on how elites and their supporters—particularly on the right—trick people into accepting ideas that benefit the rich at everyone else's expense. By using the right's talking points as a framework to explain how our political and economic system works, I hope to expose some of the ideological barriers we need to overcome if we hope to make the world livable for future generations, and in the meantime bring about meaningful improvements to people's lives.

But why even engage with the right's arguments? Doesn't the right make their arguments in bad faith? Aren't they just trying to manipulate people in order to gain power, enrich themselves, or protect the material gains they've already won? Is the right even interested in truth or reason? Can't the right just gain support by appealing to white identity, nationalism, racism, fear, and resentment? Doesn't the right only respect logic insofar as they can use it to trick people into accepting inequality and injustice? Wouldn't dunking on the right's arguments be a waste of time, which would be better focused on convincing people to support policies that benefit them, organizing communities, and getting people to the polls to take power away from the right and place it into their own hands?

These are fair questions. The right's arguments *are* often made in bad faith in order to trick people into letting the rich keep more of society's wealth. And the most effective way that poor and working class people have made gains to this point have come about through grassroots political mobilization and labor organizing, not sitting around "winning arguments" with the right. There's no substitute for the efforts of activists and organizers. But this doesn't mean we should ignore the right's arguments. When we cede ideological ground to the right, their bogus ideas become more widespread, causing millions of people to hold incorrect beliefs about how America's political and economic system works, and as a result undermine democracy, which requires an educated public in order to function. Liberals and leftists should be prepared to make sound arguments in response to right-wing propaganda, and help inoculate others from the right-wing mind virus.

Many liberals and leftists, however, *don't* know the arguments. They might *happen* to be correct to think the right's arguments are flawed, but too often they don't know *why* (or at least don't know how to articulate why). When they're confronted with the right's arguments, rather than responding in a rational manner, they're often dismissive, combative, or taken aback—unable to find a rational foothold upon which to formulate a convincing counter-argument. This allows the right to paint their targets as naive, unrealistic, "bleeding heart" saps who don't understand "how the world works," and gives the impression that the right's ideas are possibly correct. We should therefore do everything we can to neutralize the right's arguments and convince others to help make the world a better place, rather than allow right-wing propaganda to remain unchecked in the service of power and privilege. I hope this book can provide a modest contribution to that effort.

I've organized the chapters that follow around eight themes, each representing a different flavor of right-wing thought. Many on the right, for example, claim to be "conservatives." They portray themselves as responsible stewards who aim to protect society from itself. If social change moves too fast, according to conservatives, we risk political and social instability, which will lead to tyranny at the hands of the government. Conservatives claim we can avert catastrophe by adhering to certain principles, such as protecting "traditional rights" and "property rights," opposing "radical social transformation" and "judicial activism," and favoring "meritocracy." To adhere to these principles, we should allow change to come about piecemeal, through voluntary action within a capitalist economy, not by using the government to force change upon society and ensure "equal outcomes" for everyone.

In Chapter One I show why adhering to so-called conservative principles does none of these things. Conservatives support an economic system that has always destroyed traditional rights, as well as transformed society for millions of people, and continues to do so. But it does so for people who don't count in the eyes of the right—Native Americans who were dispossessed of land so white settlers could establish a system of property ownership across the American continent, slaves who were torn from their land to pick the cotton that fueled the Industrial Revolution, whites in the South who were deprived of farmland by slave owners and speculators, homesteaders in Appalachia who had their land destroyed by coal and timber companies, or manufacturing workers who've seen their jobs shipped overseas or replaced by machines in recent decades, to name a few. Capitalism transformed entire societies, and continues to create widespread poverty and misery for millions. These destructive social transformations were made possible by activist judges who made rulings on behalf of the privileged over the needs of workers and communities. These judges helped distribute society's wealth to capitalists, then insulated the resulting distribution of wealth from public control, with zero regard for how this distribution harms society. Conservatives then take the claims of the privileged—who feel they're entitled to keep the wealth they accumulate under this system—and conflate these claims with "property rights." This makes it seem as if "redistributing" property violates individual rights. But the opposite is true.

Others on the right claim to be "classical liberals." They supposedly share values with revered historical figures, such as John Locke and Adam Smith, who many celebrate for their defense of "individual liberty." Modern "classical liberals" on the right claim to share these values by opposing taxation and redistribution. If we favored individual liberty, according to the right, we'd allow individuals to keep the "fruits of their labor," favor "free markets," and allow the economy to be guided by the "invisible hand" of the market, not the hand of an all-powerful government.

In Chapter Two I show why any similarities between the modern right and classical liberals are superficial. The right's preferred economic institutions offer freedom for the privileged, while violating the individual liberty of vast swaths of the population. The claim that market income is the same as the "fruits of one's labor" is a trick meant to gain support for these institutions. The right's brand of "free market" capitalism is predicated on wild imbalances of economic and political power, which force the least advantaged into exploitative economic relationships. Rather than being guided by the "invisible hand" of the market, the economy is guided by institutions that distribute resources into the hands of the privileged, who use their power to siphon off society's wealth and corrupt the government.

Others on the right claim to be "constitutionalists." They claim we should heed the wisdom of the Constitution's framers, who aimed to create "small government" in order to limit oppression. This requires that we understand the "original intent" of the Framers. According to this doctrine, the government is limited to powers specifically enumerated in the Constitution. None of these powers allow for the types of government programs liberals and the left aim to implement, according to the right. The fact that these limitations often run counter to the idea of democracy shouldn't concern us. Like the Framers, the right claims to favor a "republican" form of government, which they say is superior to democracy because it supposedly goes further to prevent the government from violating individual rights.

In Chapter Three I show why the right's arguments in favor of "limited government"—and against democracy—fail. The aim of the Constitution was to drastically expand federal power in order to foster economic development, which the Framers believed would turn the US into a world power. It's true that the Framers attempted to erect barriers against democratic majorities, but this doesn't mean majorities can't use the powers established by the Constitution should these barriers prove insufficient. Indeed, a republic and a democracy aren't mutually exclusive concepts. A republic can lean democratic, or it can lean towards aristocracy. The right just prefers the latter, whereby economic and political power reside in the hands of a plutocracy. Under this form of republican government, corporations and the rich use their power to undermine the rights of everyone else.

Others on the right claim to favor "capitalism," which they say offers the most freedom of any economic system. We should stick with "free trade" and "free markets," which have not only lifted billions of people out of poverty, but are the only ways countries can develop and enjoy economic prosperity in the long run. According to the right, deviating from free trade and free markets will lead to mass murder and starvation (see the Soviet Union under Stalin and China under Mao), if not fascism—which the right claims is a left-wing phenomenon. To see a contemporary example, look to Venezuela. If we adopt left-wing policies, we'll soon be eating rats for dinner! While the right admits that capitalism isn't without problems, they say we shouldn't kill the goose that lays the golden eggs. Any problems with capitalism are just "crony capitalism," which results from government intervention in the economy, not capitalism itself. It follows that the solution is less government, not less capitalism.

In Chapter Four I show why capitalism has not only failed to deliver on the promises of its supporters, but causes untold misery and destruction. "Free trade" is a form of pillage that dates back centuries. The major capitalist powers only began to advocate "free trade" after they developed by doing the opposite. These countries used state intervention to establish a competitive advantage over less-developed countries, then realized they benefited if other countries adopted free trade, because this provides developed countries access to new markets, cheap labor, and raw materials, which boost corporate profits. Free trade, however, has destroyed the lives of millions of people in less-developed countries. Nor has any country ever descended into totalitarianism by adopting the types of left-wing reforms advocated by the right's opponents. Nearly all developed countries except for the US have created large welfare states, yet remain among the freest and most prosperous in the world. But if we're keeping score, I'll show that the communist regimes led by Stalin and Mao can't hold a candle to the devastation unleashed by capitalist regimes.

Others on the right claim that liberals and the left don't understand how the economy works. If they did, they'd know that efforts by the government to fix social problems like poverty are futile. Indeed, some claim that poverty isn't a problem at all. Just look at all the poor people who have cell phones and microwaves! To the degree poverty *is* a problem, it *wouldn't* be if individuals weren't mired in a "culture of poverty" that turns them into lazy bums who mooch off the rest of society instead of "getting a job." Nor is it a problem that income has stagnated for much of the American middle class, according to the right, who points out that the *upper*-middle class has expanded in recent decades. More importantly, even if we wanted to redistribute wealth to fix problems like poverty and income stagnation, the right maintains that this is impossible. Eventually we'll run out of money, living standards will decline, and everyone will be made worse off. The right claims that the only reason other countries are able to implement expansive public safety nets is because they have a number of advantages we don't have in the US.

In Chapter Five I show why poverty and income stagnation are indeed major problems in the US. Poverty creates stress, insecurity, and stigmatization for millions of people—including children—and limits their human potential. I'll also show that a robust social welfare state is the most effective means by which we can reduce poverty and income inequality. These programs have enjoyed widespread success all over the world, including in the US. The reason the US hasn't made more headway against problems like poverty—and middle-class incomes have stagnated—is because economic elites have structured our economy in a way that distributes society's resources to themselves. Elites leave the rest of society without sufficient means, while doing everything they can to undermine America's welfare state.

Others on the right claim to value "personal responsibility." They downplay the historical legacies of past institutions, such as slavery and discrimination, pointing out that slavery ended over 150 years ago, and that Jim Crow ended over 50 years ago. Traditionally oppressed minorities, such as blacks, have therefore had plenty of time to catch up to whites, according to the right. We're told that problems like "institutional racism" are just a lame excuse for those who refuse to pick themselves up by their own bootstraps.

In Chapter Six I show that institutional racism remains a problem in the US. We're only a few generations removed from the end of Jim Crow, at which point blacks found themselves at the bottom of America's economic hierarchy and lacked the means by which to make sufficient gains relative to those who've traditionally benefited from how the American economy is structured. Racial bias in housing, education, employment, and the criminal justice system also persists to an unacceptable degree. More importantly, over the past several decades economic elites have been waging a one-sided class war on the poor and middle class, resulting in extreme levels of economic inequality. This disproportionately hurts blacks, due to the legacy of slavery and Jim Crow. In order to mask this reality, the right shifts blame onto individuals who are disadvantaged by our economic system, thereby avoiding any collective responsibility we have to ensure that all Americans enjoy a sufficient level of freedom and independence.

Others on the right identify as supporters of the Republican Party. They defend the Party by pointing out that Abraham Lincoln, Frederick Douglass, and Dwight Eisenhower were Republicans. Whereas the Republican Party ended slavery, and later supported civil rights laws, the right points out that the Democratic Party was once the party of slavery, segregation, and the KKK, and that a lower percentage of Democratic legislators supported civil rights laws in the 1960s than Republicans. The reason blacks support the Democratic Party despite its racist past, is because Democrats give them "free stuff" like healthcare and housing subsidies, which allows them to live on the dole, according to the right. Democrats are therefore racist, because they aim to keep blacks "enslaved" on a "liberal plantation" of welfare dependency. In contrast, the reason so many whites support the Republican Party is because they just want everyone to be able to keep their hard-earned money. Some on the right even maintain that if Martin Luther King were still alive, he would be a conservative—if not a Republican—because, like the right, he believed in "personal responsibility."

In Chapter Seven I show that while it was once true that the Republican Party could call itself the party of civil rights, this wasn't the case for long. The Party abandoned blacks, became the party of big business, and eventually destroyed the economy. This allowed Democrats to take power and offer jobs and economic relief to Americans—including blacks. By the time the Civil Rights era rolled around, the Republican Party had been largely pushed out of power, and counted a number of moderates and liberals among its ranks. Support for civil rights laws came from *these* members, who acted as junior partners with liberal Democrats when passing civil rights legislation. In the decades that followed passage of the major civil rights bills, conservatives took control of the Republican Party while ramping up efforts to court white voters who were leaving the Democratic Party in response to its support for civil rights. Republicans mixed economic and racial rhetoric to appeal to white voters while supporting policies that kept blacks cemented at the bottom of America's economic hierarchy. This fact was not lost on Martin Luther King, who understood that economic justice went hand-in-hand with racial justice, and saw perfectly well what the Republican Party was turning into before he was assassinated.

Finally, many on the right claim that liberals and the left use their power to silence right-wing views. Liberals and the left, we're told, control the media, which they use to promote a "left-wing" agenda, and use a number of nefarious tactics—enforcing political correctness, shouting down right-wing speakers on college campuses, and cajoling companies like Facebook and Google to censor right-wing views—in order to entrench their power and limit the speech of their opposition. Much of this stems from "identity politics," whose adherents reject truth in favor of "victim narratives," which liberal politicians exploit by unfairly branding their political opponents on the right as racist reactionaries.

In Chapter Eight, I expose the right's childlike understanding of how the media works. The media is not only owned by giant corporate conglomerates, but is heavily subsidized by the political, military, and business establishment. This ensures that media bias skews from center-right to right on economic issues, which are far more consequential to the lives of ordinary people than social and cultural issues having to do with political correctness and antiracism. Nor do political correctness, campus protests, and cancel culture pose a threat to free speech. Because wealth in the US is concentrated in the hands of a corporate elite, the right's ability to have their speech heard, and affect change in society, far outweighs the speech of those who attempt to "silence" the right. This will always be the case as long as the distribution of wealth in society remains unequal. I conclude by showing that the right cultivates their own form of identity politics—fueled by cable news and social media—to mobilize resentment against vulnerable groups, and distract from the right's primary goal, which is to maintain a system of social and economic inequality.

CHAPTER ONE

Conservatism

For decades the American right has branded its political movement as "conservative." Many on the right, for example, claim to value "traditional rights," oppose "radical social transformation," oppose "constitutional innovation," and believe that social inequality is a natural and permanent feature of any society. These principles have defined conservative political ideology since the writings of Edmund Burke, the so-called father of modern conservatism, who wrote in support of these principles in reaction to the French Revolution. The aim of these principles, we're told, is to "conserve" society in order to protect individual liberty. When governments violate traditional rights (in particular, what the right refers to as "property rights"), enact policies that bring about social change too rapidly, or empower judges to alter laws based on novel interpretations of written constitutions, we risk social instability. This can only end with despotism and tyranny, much like the Reign of Terror or the totalitarian political and economic systems that grew out of the Russian and Chinese revolutions.

According to a modern variant of this argument, violating property rights (for example, by raising taxes too much) also disincentivizes individuals to work hard. This erodes the social hierarchies needed for a prosperous society. If individuals have no incentive to make use of their talents, the cream can't rise to the top so to speak, and society will suffer from less innovation and we'll all have less wealth as a result. Instead of supporting higher taxes, therefore, we should reward those who put their talents to good use, and allow society to reap the economic benefits individuals create, according to the right. If social and economic hierarchies arise from this process, who cares?

In order to adhere to conservative principles, and thereby prevent the perverse outcomes left-wing policies foist upon society, the right claims we should support a conservative economic agenda. This entails less spending on social programs, lower taxes, and judicial restraint. The latter of these three pillars—judicial restraint—is key here. After all, the government can only institute expansive social programs—and the higher taxes needed to pay for these programs—when liberal judges misinterpret the Constitution, according to the right, allowing elected representatives to enact laws that exceed the proper scope of congressional authority.

In practice, however, tax cuts, less social spending, and judicial restraint have little to do with adhering to conservative principles. On the contrary, this approach to policy fuels an economic system that has always destroyed traditional rights, as well as radically transformed society for millions—and not in a good way. During the late nineteenth and early twentieth centuries, large corporations came to dominate American society. They restructured the economy, corrupted our political system, and subordinated the rights of individuals to the freedom of a moneyed elite. Indeed, as we'll see, a number of prominent conservatives who witnessed these social transformations unfold over a century ago understood this perfectly and made their concerns known. Modern "conservatives," on the other hand, favor a brand of unfettered capitalism that concentrates economic and political power into the hands of corporations and their owners, allowing these interests to wreak havoc on society.

We'll also see that capitalism couldn't have destroyed traditional rights or radically transformed society without the help of activist judges. These judges invented new law on behalf of capitalists in the name of "progress," which they equated with economic development. The laws they helped establish limited the power of workers and insulated capitalists from democratic control, which bestowed elites with the power to appropriate the bulk of society's wealth, leaving millions without the resources necessary to enjoy a sufficient level of individual freedom and autonomy. Conservatives' defense of "property rights" should be understood in this context. Elites constantly rig our economic and political system to distribute society's wealth to themselves—primarily with the aid of the courts—and have done so for hundreds of years. Conservatives want us to ignore this history so they can trick the rest of society into letting economic elites keep the property they steal from the rest of society.

The same is true of conservatives' defense of social hierarchies that arise from capitalism. Conservatives claim that those who rise through the ranks of society do so on the basis of "merit." They achieve success by "working hard" and taking advantage of the opportunities life provides them. This claim is especially powerful and widely accepted—including among liberals, who are some of its most ardent defenders. But as we'll see, the social hierarchies that arise from capitalism have much more to do with the way we structure our political and economic institutions.

Traditional Rights

Conservatives claim to value "traditional rights." Conservative commentator Mark Levin, for example, uses the idea of traditional rights to differentiate conservatism from the left. Levin claims that the left justifies its policies as conferring "new, abstract rights"—for example, the right to healthcare or the right to a job—but that these rights are "nothing more than a Statist deception intended to empower the state and deny man his real rights—those that are both inalienable and anchored in custom, tradition, and faith."[1] But Levin has it backwards. Access to healthcare and jobs protects traditional rights, whereas the right aims to deny man his rights, and uses the state to this end. In order to understand why, it's helpful to look at how elites have deprived ordinary people of rights throughout history.

The types of rights favored by the left are hardly new or abstract. While "jobs" haven't always been thought of as a right, and healthcare as we know it today obviously hasn't always existed, the right to access enough of society's resources to live, given the resources available, has long been recognized. In pre-capitalist societies, peasants had the right to the commons—land upon which they could hunt and gather food to feed their families, collect wood to build and heat their homes, and graze livestock to produce additional food and clothing. These rights were outlined in the Charter of the Forest, a companion document to Magna Carta, and enforced for hundreds of years. In an otherwise brutal world, the right to the commons allowed ordinary people some degree of independence from the hands of their rulers. Peasants had to give the lord a share of what they produced, but they were able to work under their own direction to produce for their own needs, without an overseer's constant supervision.²

Eventually, a new aristocracy had other ideas about the commons and used "property rights" to swallow up much of the peasantry's sliver of independence. As capitalism began to replace feudalism in parts of Europe, elites *privatized* the commons. They converted the commons into large-scale farms to produce crops and raw materials for commercial gain, and prohibited peasants from accessing the commons under penalty of death. Because a small minority of aristocrats exercised absolute ownership rights over the bulk of society's wealth, ordinary people were dispossessed of the means to live and forced into a permanent state of dependence.³ Thomas Jefferson was among those acknowledging the injustice wrought by this form of dispossession. Writing of one of his visits to France in the years preceding the French Revolution, Jefferson observed, "Whenever there is in any country, uncultivated lands and unemployed poor, it is clear that the laws of property have been so far extended as to violate natural right. The earth is given as a common stock for man to labour and live on."⁴

This doesn't mean people fared better under feudalism. Living standards have of course improved over the past 200 years. But as we'll see, there has always been a tension between traditional rights and the type of economic system the right favors, due to the social relationships that form in capitalist economies. Note Jefferson's reference to the "laws of property." While conservatives claim that the left uses the state to violate individual rights (by redistributing property), this is in fact the primary means by which the right violates individual rights. Once the state creates legal institutions that confer ownership over the resources individuals need to survive, and these resources become scarce (for example, because those with more power are able to appropriate the resources), those who don't own enough resources must work for those who do. Owners then use their control over resources to dominate those with less, thereby violating their rights. The reason they can do this is because they rely on the state to enforce a distribution of property that creates the conditions for domination.

Jefferson went on to compare the conditions in France to those in the United States at the time, observing, "It is too soon yet in our country to say that every man who cannot find employment but who can find uncultivated land, shall be at liberty to cultivate it, paying a moderate rent. But it is not too soon to provide by every possible means that as few as possible shall be without a little portion of land. The small landholders are the most precious part of a state."[5] In other words when Jefferson commented on the conditions in France, American elites had yet to achieve the same level of power as their French counterparts, because they had yet to appropriate as much of society's wealth (in this case, land). The conditions Jefferson described, however, would over time give way to dispossession.

Elites dispossessed the rest of society in a variety of ways. In the antebellum South, wealthy planters bought up the best land in order to produce tobacco and cotton. This forced smaller farmers to live on the worst land, which created widespread poverty. This appropriation of resources was followed by a century of underdevelopment, which deprived most people of the resources needed thrive (for example, a quality education). As a result, when compared to the rest of the country, the South remains poor to this day.[6]

The same is true of Appalachia. After the Civil War, coal and timber companies bought up enormous tracts of land, which they often procured using political connections. Homesteaders had their land sold out from under them, while resource extraction eroded these homesteaders' soil and poisoned their water. Many were forced into wage labor working for these companies, which paid them next to nothing. The companies used their wealth to corrupt every level of government; they effectively owned the towns where they operated, or literally created "company towns," where they controlled nearly every aspect of their workers' lives. This imbalance of power allowed owners to appropriate the wealth workers created, leaving much of the region underdeveloped.[7]

In the Midwest, elites used debt to dispossess smaller farmers, who increasingly had to borrow in order to secure land, or had to produce larger yields in order to repay this debt. This left them vulnerable to crop failures, natural disasters, and competition with larger enterprises as markets enveloped American society, often giving them little choice but to sell their farms to those with more wealth.[8]

In America's industrial centers, large business enterprises dispossessed their workers. Economies of scale limited opportunities for self-employment, while waves of immigration expanded the labor supply, forcing workers into fiercer competition with each other.[9] To protect themselves from these conditions, workers attempted to form labor unions, which would have allowed them to bargain with employers for better pay and safer working conditions. In response, they were met with violence and repression at the hands of their employers, not to mention the government, which intervened in these disputes on the employers' behalf.[10]

These forms of dispossession are mild compared to what Native Americans and blacks endured. Tens of thousands (if not hundreds of thousands) of Native Americans were killed by white settlers, had their land stolen, or were herded onto reservations. Blacks of course found themselves literally defined as the property of whites, precluding any possibility that they might own land and become independent farmers. Even after slavery was abolished, whites maintained ownership of the land and enforced Black Codes, which forced blacks into exploitative labor contracts that mirrored slavery.[11] After Reconstruction, whites imposed Jim Crow laws, which deprived blacks of access to education and public accommodations, keeping them cemented at the bottom of America's class hierarchy. When blacks migrated to northern cities to escape these oppressive conditions, they faced discrimination, were relegated to the worst jobs, and were paid less than their white counterparts.[12] When they attempted to join forces with whites and demand higher pay and better working conditions, employers deindustrialized, or started outsourcing jobs to the South, where laws were more favorable to employers, or to developing countries.[13]

The legacy of these forms of dispossession remains with us today. When a child is born into a segregated inner-city or suburb, or a holler in West Virginia, or a Native American reservation in Oklahoma, and as a result must grow up surrounded by poverty, violence, drugs, and crime, or without access to quality education, housing, and healthcare, and therefore lacks sufficient opportunity to realize their human potential, it's because elites throughout history structured America's political and economic system to deprive others of adequate resources, and continue to do so.

Over the last five decades, elites have employed a number of tactics to continually dispossess workers and their families. They've weakened unions, let the minimum wage erode, used monetary policy to generate unemployment, slashed public jobs, and cut welfare programs, while continuing to offshore jobs to developing countries. These policies relegate millions to undesirable jobs with little prospect of long-term economic security or income mobility. Most workers no longer have the power to bargain for a larger slice of America's economic pie in order to support their families, and are left to endure workplace indignities—like harassment from bosses, lack of control over their work, and being cut out of key decisions that affect their job. Elites have also used the wealth they accumulate on the backs of workers to corrupt our political system and help elect politicians that cut their taxes, shower them with subsidies, deregulate industry, and curb voting rights in order to help them gain an electoral advantage.[14]

Women face additional obstacles. They didn't have the right to vote until 1920 and were largely excluded from the formal labor force until World War II. Indeed, employment levels for women didn't reach parity with men until the 1990s. To this day, women must bear the brunt of responsibility for household production (cooking, cleaning, laundry, etc.), for which they receive no income; as well as child-rearing, which often sets their careers on different trajectories than their male counterparts.[15]

Undocumented immigrants face even harder challenges. Many come from countries colonized by European powers that prevented economic development, enclosed commons, poisoned the environment, and undercut farmers' livelihoods by flooding local markets with cheap produce. Under the rule of western-backed, authoritarian regimes, peasants had their liberties repressed and were deprived of democratic political institutions that might have allowed them to structure their economies in a way that benefited ordinary people. When undocumented immigrants from these countries arrive in America, the injustice continues. They lack many of the rights of American citizens, are excluded from access to social programs like Social Security, and have little choice but to find work in dangerous factories, agricultural labor camps, or low-paid service industries. If they raise their voice or try to organize, they can be threatened with deportation.[16]

If so-called conservatives were serious about defending traditional rights, they would acknowledge the history outlined above and view the wealth that flows to the privileged as an ongoing form of dispossession. We should all view this wealth as the modern equivalent of the "uncultivated lands" to which Thomas Jefferson referred, and therefore distribute this wealth as we see fit instead of allowing the rich to hoard it for themselves or use it as a lever by which to wring ever more wealth from the powerless. We could, for example, use some of this wealth to create a robust welfare state, which might provide everyone with enough resources to enjoy a sufficient level of freedom.

Contrary to what conservatives claim, social welfare programs aren't a "Statist deception" intended to deny man his traditional rights. On the contrary, these programs are the most effective institutions we've established to prevent traditional rights from being annihilated. They provide individuals with the resources needed to live free of control by elites who do everything they can to dominate society. If healthcare isn't tied to employment, childcare is provided, elderly people are guaranteed income, college is accessible without accruing tens or hundreds of thousands of dollars of debt, and workers can easily join unions, people are less dependent on their employers, and therefore less subject to their employer's control. Expanding social welfare policies helps to restore the function traditional rights once served—until those rights were continually destroyed by the right's brand of "free market" capitalism.

Conservatives don't care about traditional rights. What they care about is privileging the rights of the wealthy to enrich themselves, even if it means denying the traditional rights of those who get in their way.

Radical Social Transformation

Conservatives claim to oppose "radical social transformation." They argue that tax hikes and redistributive social welfare programs will give too much power to the government, transform society, and pave the way for anarchy, despotism, and tyranny. Instead, they say we should keep taxes low and redistribution to a minimum and allow social change to happen piecemeal through voluntary economic exchange in a capitalist economy. What conservatives ignore, however, is how capitalism was—and continues to be—forced on society through radical, often violent, social transformation.

As capitalism took off in the nineteenth century, new prospects for securing natural resources and new markets to sell goods drove territorial expansion across the North American continent. In the process, American settlers, as well as the US Army, slaughtered thousands of Native Americans. They killed thousands more by spreading disease and herded the rest onto reservations. Similarly, in the decades preceding the Civil War, growing demand for cotton fueled the expansion of slavery, which helped develop America's capitalist economy.[17] This violent history poses a problem for conservatives, who claim that capitalism requires little more than leaving individuals free to engage in voluntary economic exchange in the "free market." It's clear, however, that when conservatives refer to "individuals," they don't mean slaves or Native Americans that lived during the period capitalism took root in the US. Conservatives therefore oppose radical social transformation for some people, but not others.

It would be one thing if conservatives acknowledged the role that slavery, theft, and genocide played in establishing their preferred economic system, and took steps to ensure capitalism doesn't harm vulnerable populations moving forward. Instead, conservatives deny any such role, and promote an agenda that continues to brutalize people all over the world to expand the reach of capital. Whether this means slaughtering millions of peasants in Korea, Vietnam, and Cambodia;[18] outsourcing murder and torture to authoritarian dictatorships in the name of anticommunism;[19] or supporting trade policies that allow US corporations to destroy peasant societies—by kicking people off their land, poisoning their environments, or even hiring death squads to murder them—conservatives remain blind to many forms of radical social transformation wrought by their preferred economic policies.[20] This is enough to reject the idea that conservatives are concerned with the effects of radical social transformation.

But it turns out that conservatives' opposition to radical social transformation is even more limited. Capitalism also radically transformed society for those who don't happen to have black or brown skin, or live out of view halfway around the world. For centuries, those who lived in America's traditional farming communities worked alongside their neighbors in grist mills, blacksmith shops, tanneries, and sawmills to meet their needs. These communities balanced their productive capabilities, and residents exchanged labor with each other depending on where it was most needed. They built each other's houses and barns, cut logs, harvested wheat, and so on. If one person accrued a debt, this debt wasn't calculated as money owed, but as labor—to be paid back only when one could do so. Nor did laborers depend on employers for their long-term survival. When relying on labor markets, workers could demand high wages, since labor was relatively scarce. This was a temporary step towards independence, which was all but assured, given that labor markets worked in their favor. The rapid expansion of the market economy throughout the nineteenth century, however, transformed the nature of these social relationships.[21]

Capitalism replaced traditional social relationships based on kinship, religion, and barter exchange with impersonal, commercial relationships based on property rights and contracts. As capitalism enveloped American society, artisans and farmers who once produced for themselves under their own direction, along with laborers who could once demand high wages, were increasingly forced to work for larger manufacturers under unfavorable terms to earn money. Many moved into company housing and became subject to closer supervision. Workers were forced to increase output to produce greater profits for factory owners while their own wages were continually slashed.[22]

Those who found their lives subject to new forms of control bitterly resented these transformations. As historian Charles Sellers points out, some worried that capital would "swallow up the profits of labor," that the people would be "pillaged by the greedy cupidity of a privileged class," and that the "manufacturing monopolies" would "break down the independent mechanic interest," and "make large masses of people" eke out "a bare subsistence" as "slaves to a few capitalists."[23] These transformations would drastically accelerate with the arrival of the Industrial Revolution—business enterprises grew larger, economies of scale further limited opportunities for self-employment, economic power became concentrated in the hands of large employers, and social relations between economic classes became more stratified.[24]

These transformations were far from piecemeal or orderly. When workers attempted to resist capitalist social transformation (for example, by forming labor unions), employers mobilized private police forces, as well as the state, to destroy them. Detective agencies like Pinkerton and Baldwin-Felts beat up workers, kicked them out of their houses, spied on them, and even murdered them.[25] Despite these violent tactics, workers won many victories. The eight-hour work day, the five-day work week, workplace safety regulations, the minimum wage, unemployment insurance, Social Security, and collective bargaining rights can all be credited to workers who fought back against capitalist social transformation.[26] These programs weren't an attempt to radically transform society, but a reaction to the rise of corporate power in the wake of the Industrial Revolution and later the Great Depression.[27]

The struggle continues today against five decades of economic reforms that have eroded the power of the middle class and ensure persistently high levels of poverty. De-industrialization, industrial automation, declining union membership, higher levels of unemployment, slashes to social spending, trade agreements, lax antitrust law, lower taxes for the wealthy, the erosion of the minimum wage, slashes to public education, right-to-work laws, deregulation—the list goes on. These policies have destroyed countless communities that once relied on good manufacturing jobs, as well destroyed the economic ladder by which those at the bottom of America's economic hierarchy once lifted themselves into the middle class.[28]

Indeed, it's difficult to see how modern reforms proposed by the left are more radical. Bumping the minimum wage to $15 or $20 per hour, or doing what every other rich country has already done—for example, providing health insurance to its citizens—wouldn't radically transform society. On the contrary, it's conservatives who wish to radically transform society—back to the way it was before the New Deal, when corporations had even less accountability, economic inequality was at its peak, and the economy was plagued by financial instability.

In many ways, capitalist transformation would go much further—by ensuring the worst outcomes scientists predict will arise from climate change, which threaten to kill millions of people around the world and fundamentally transform human civilization. It follows that policies such as a Green New Deal wouldn't so much transform society as provide the bare minimum needed to prevent enormous losses of human life, as well prevent as social collapse.[29] So-called conservatives don't have a problem with radical social transformation. They only have a problem with transformations that might alter the balance of power in society between the rich and everyone else, even if it means destroying the entire planet.

Judicial Activism

Conservatives claim to oppose "judicial activism." When liberal judges uphold "unconstitutional" laws, such as those establishing social welfare programs like Obamacare, conservatives claim this erodes the "rule of law," gives too much power to the government, and thereby opens the door for tyranny. Conservatives, however, ignore the role judicial activism has played in establishing the right's brand of "free market" capitalism. Since the early nineteenth century, judicial activism has continually structured "free markets" in a way that distributes society's wealth to its most privileged members, and shields this wealth from being redistributed.

An early example of judicial activism took place in 1823 when the Supreme Court ruled in *Johnson v. M'Intosh* that white people had priority rights to newly "discovered" land, superseding claims by mere "occupants" of the land. This allowed Congress to pass the Indian Removal Act of 1830, which gave the government legal sanction to slaughter thousands of Native Americans, steal their land, and herd the rest onto reservations.[30] Judicial activism therefore created the legal basis for theft on behalf of white people, and along with it the system of property rights that would extend across the nation.

The courts would not only help distribute society's wealth to white people, but they would do so disproportionately to new commercial enterprises. They did this by reinterpreting the nature of property rights and contracts. Let's say, for example, that you lived near a waterway during the early nineteenth century. A mill owner then builds a dam downstream from you, flooding your property. It used to be that you could sue the mill owner for violating your property rights. The courts, however, started changing the law in favor of new mill owners, based on the idea that economic development benefited the public, and that this fact trumped the importance of traditional notions of property rights.[31]

In order to get a better idea as to why these rulings constituted a form of judicial activism, it's important to point out that when judges began to make rulings like these, the nature of institutions such as property rights weren't always clear. While nearly everyone agreed that the government should protect "property rights," what constituted property rights in the first place was far from settled. Should we respect the claims of Native Americans to their land? Should we confiscate property held by British Loyalists after the Revolutionary War? Should states be allowed to enact debtor relief laws and issue paper currency? Should the government honor the full value of bonds bought on speculation? And so on.

Several of the Founders took a relatively left-wing view on some of these matters. Thomas Jefferson thought that if the distribution of property in society were to become highly skewed, this would violate the "natural rights" of those without property, and might call for the "laws of property" to be changed.[32] Benjamin Franklin believed individuals were only entitled to own property sufficient to "conserve the individual," and that society may "dispose of the rest as it wished."[33] Thomas Paine wrote that society must be organized "like a system of pulleys" in order to relieve human misery, and to this end advocated state-funded old age pensions and lump sum payments to all citizens upon reaching adulthood, to be administered by the state and funded by an estate tax.[34]

The courts, however, would create their own system of pulleys. Rather than interpret the law to relieve human misery, they did so in a way that privileged the power of capital. In *Dartmouth v. Woodward* (1819), the Court ruled that state-granted charters were a type of "contract," and were therefore protected by the Constitution. As a result, corporations would be free from state regulation beyond what was stipulated in their charters. This was significant because corporate charters had traditionally been understood as artificial creations of the state, and were subject to regulation or amendment by the state that issued them. And for good reason. It was well understood that corporations were often established to enrich the well-connected, and if allowed, would act counter to the public interest. This is why charters often limited corporations to specific functions, were set to expire after a specified length of time, and capped the amount of profit corporations could make.[35] This isn't to say the *Dartmouth* ruling automatically freed corporations from regulation. States did, after all, include regulatory provisions in corporate charters. But as we'll see, *Dartmouth* foreshadowed a number of judicial rulings that would suit the changing needs of capitalists, and eventually allow corporate power to grow unchecked.

One such ruling was *Charles River Bridge v. Warren Bridge* (1837), in which the US Supreme Court held that incumbent investors might no longer be entitled to the monopoly privileges implied in a corporation's charter. In this case, investors who had a stake in an existing bridge claimed the government broke its contract when constructing a new bridge. The Court held, however, that if such privileges would hold back economic development (which might result from new competition, for example), old legal interpretations were to be cast aside.[36] It turns out that whether a corporate charter constituted a contract was up for debate, depending on the situation. According to legal scholar Morton Horwitz, these types of innovations arose because judges came to see themselves not as neutral arbiters applying traditional interpretations of the law, but as agents for social progress, which they equated with economic development.[37]

This isn't to say that judicial activism meant to promote economic development was all bad. It's true that the public often benefited from competition when markets worked the way their proponents claim. But markets often *didn't* work this way, and economic progress was narrowly defined in terms of how much wealth commercial enterprise produced. Questions regarding the distribution of this wealth—between capitalists and workers, for example—would be left to the market, where capitalists enjoyed a great deal of power, and workers—along with the broader public—would find themselves with hardly any. Given this reality, judicial activism would come to arbitrarily favor capitalists.

The arbitrary nature of judicial activism is evident by the way the courts interpreted the relationship between employers and employees. While the courts innovated new commercial law in order to foster "progress," when it came to labor practices, courts often based their rulings on feudal precedents. If an individual agreed to work for an employer for a certain length of time, for example, they would only be entitled to compensation if they completed the entire duration specified at the outset of the labor agreement. If the employee became injured, or wished to walk away from the job before the end of the contract, rather than being entitled to compensation for the work performed to that point, the courts held that the employee would be entitled to nothing. But when it came to businesses contracting with each other, the courts interpreted the law much differently. If a builder had performed work for another business, but couldn't complete the job to the specifications outlined in the work contract, the builder would still be entitled to compensation.[38]

Judicial activism afforded employers a great deal of power over their employees. Employers could cheat workers out of their pay by waiting until the end of the employment period, then claim the employee had failed to perform some part of his duties, and use this claim as a basis to terminate the contract. This isn't to say employers always used this tactic, but the threat that they could do so served as a deterrent to employees from ending a contract with an employer, and impeded labor mobility.[39] When workers tried to push back against these forms of control—by organizing labor unions or participating in strikes—judges often intervened on behalf of employers, issuing labor injunctions to put a stop to these strikes.[40]

Judges who innovated in this way tried to have it both ways. In the pre-capitalist apprentice systems found in Europe, masters were obligated to provide their apprentices with housing, food, clothing, tools, and so on. They were liable for their apprentices' mistakes and were expected to honor these duties for years, at which point the apprentice would become a master himself. Once the apprentice became a master, he joined a guild, which offered him economic security. This type of relationship became anachronistic in America during its colonial period and the first decades after US independence, as laborers had access to cheap land (at least if they were white), which enabled them to produce for their own needs or demand high wages. While many immigrants came to America as indentured servants, for the most part laborers were unencumbered by the types of social relationships found in feudal guild systems. As America's economy developed, however, labor markets came to favor employers at the expense of laborers. Land became more scarce. High birth rates, along with waves of immigration, dramatically expanded the labor pool. Workers were forced into labor markets, where they increasingly had less power, and as a result became subject to economic exploitation at the hands of corporations. Rather than take these factors into account and update the law in order to secure workers a sufficient level of freedom, judges continued to idealize labor contracts as voluntary associations between free individuals—with each party owing the other little beyond what they contractually agreed upon. These rulings served to reinforce extreme levels of inequality that arose from America's rapidly developing economy.[41]

These developments led to warnings from a number of dissenting voices—even among conservative legal authorities. Legal scholar Christopher Tiedeman warned that if corporate power were left unchecked, this would "be a menace to the liberty of the individual, and to the stability of the American States as popular governments," that the establishment of corporate charters served to "intensify the natural power which the capitalist in his individual capacity possesses over the noncapitalist," and therefore advocated "as a return to a uniform recognition of the constitutional guarantee of equality before the law, the repeal of the statutes which provide for the creation of private corporations."[42] Chief Justice of the Michigan Supreme Court Thomas Cooley claimed that "the most enormous and threatening powers in our country have been created; some of the great and wealthy corporations have greater influence in the country at large and upon the legislation of the country than the States to which they owe their corporate existence."[43] Likewise, Elihu Root, Theodore Roosevelt's eventual Secretary of State, described corporate campaign contributions as "the constantly growing evil in our political affairs, which has, in my judgment, done more to shake the confidence of the plain people of small means in our political institutions, than any other practice which has ever obtained since the foundation of our government."[44]

Instead of using the law to limit the power of corporations, the courts would continue to do everything possible to insulate corporations from democratic politics. State courts invalidated laws that limited work hours. The Supreme Court ruled that corporations could seek federal enforcement of agreements made when operating outside of the state in which they were chartered, that corporations would enjoy the protection of federal judicial review of state legislatures, that corporations could often ignore the decisions of state regulatory commissions, that states couldn't pass laws banning "yellow dog" contracts, that it was legal to jail anyone who joined radical organizations like the IWW, and that the so-called rights of shareholders must be respected above the interests of workers, as well as those who lived in the communities in which corporations operated.[45]

Some of these legal innovations were truly astonishing. After the states ratified the 14th Amendment, which aimed to protect the rights of former slaves, the Court all but ignored the rights of black people and instead used the Amendment's Equal Protection Clause to shield shareholders from legislation that might diminish the value of their holdings without due process.[46] The Court also protected corporations from the Sherman Anti-Trust Act, maintaining that combinations of capital were legal unless they were "unreasonable," providing judges with wiggle room when applying the law to regulate commercial enterprises, while using the Act to crush labor unions, which the courts characterized as "combinations" of labor analogous to corporate monopolies.[47]

The distributive effects of these judicial decisions can't be understated. Because capital was encouraged to combine indefinitely—while workers were limited in the extent to which they could organize—workers found themselves without the power to bargain for higher wages and better working conditions. As a result, they were left with a smaller share of the economic gains derived from what they produced. Judicial activism thereby helped funnel wealth into the pockets of capitalists and out of the pockets of ordinary Americans, helping to fuel extreme levels of economic inequality.

Judicial activism hasn't all been in one direction. During the Great Depression, President Roosevelt threatened to pack the Supreme Court with judges who were sympathetic to his economic agenda, forcing the Court to change its interpretation on the constitutionality of several laws, thereby granting more power to workers and allowing the government to regulate work hours and wages on workers' behalf, and eventually regulate workplace safety, as well as pass environmental regulations.[48] The Warren Court put a formal end to segregation in public schools, expanding educational opportunities for blacks in the 1950s, and signaled it would do the same for the poor more generally.[49]

Since the 1970s, however, the Court has lurched back to the right. Richard Nixon packed the Court, flipping the Court's ideological balance, after which the Court halted school integration, denied equal state funding for schools, defined money as a form of speech, intervened in the 2000 presidential election to install Republican candidate George W. Bush as President (and ensured the Court would remain conservative), allowed corporations to spend unlimited resources on elections, overturned Section 5 of the Voting Rights Act, and so on. These rulings have helped conservatives maintain an outsized influence on American politics, which they've used to continue funneling more of society's wealth to themselves.[50]

If conservatives really opposed judicial activism, they would acknowledge this history, and admit that judicial activism has always been intrinsic to the nature of the judicial branch and that any judicial decision along the lines outlined here always has distributional effects when it comes to income and wealth. Instead, so-called conservatives pretend their interpretations of the law are neutral, and ignore judicial activism when it's used to rig the economic and political system in favor of power and privilege.

Property Rights

When conservatives oppose what they consider high levels of taxation, they often do so on the basis of defending "property rights." Commentator Mark Levin, when responding to the prospect of a tax hike supported by then-president Barack Obama, worried that Obama was "completely rejecting the notion of private property rights."[51] The way conservatives use the term "property rights," however, is misleading. When we pass a law to raise taxes, it doesn't allow me to squat in your house, sleep in your bed, or drive your car around town without your permission when you're not using it. Taxation might bring about a different *distribution* of property, but we still have laws that protect everyone's property once we decide how it should be distributed.

Conservatives' conception of property rights differs from how the rest of the world defines property rights, which are merely legal institutions that societies establish through their governments to enforce property ownership. Conservatives instead conflate their ideas about *who should own what property* with property rights itself. They think property acquisition arising within the market is just; therefore those who engage in market exchange have a "right" to whatever property they can acquire in this way. In other words, they should be morally entitled to keep this property.

The problem with this conception of property rights is that those who acquire property in the so-called free market often *shouldn't* be entitled to keep this property. One reason for this is that market exchange often isn't just. This happens when one party to an economic exchange enjoys a great deal more power than another party, and uses this imbalance of power to take advantage of the weaker party. Let's say you're a worker who needs to feed your family or pay next month's rent. You take a job working at Walmart because you have few other options. If you want to bargain for higher wages and benefits, or better working conditions, good luck. You're bargaining on Walmart's terms. They don't need you as much as you need them. As a result, you make less and they make more—and it doesn't matter if you think you're getting screwed. Indeed, those who view such an exchange as unjust can raise the same objections conservatives do about taxation. If "property rights" just means "whatever property we think we're entitled to," then market exchange that results in a distribution of property we think is unjust violates the "property rights" of those who get taken advantage of.

One might be tempted to think that distributing property through markets is fundamentally different than distributing property via the tax system, because taxation involves coercion at the hands of the government whereas market exchange doesn't. But this isn't true. When individuals engage in market exchange, they always do so within a set of state-enforced legal constraints that lurk in the background. These constraints are what underpin the bargaining power of those who engage in market exchange, and allow those in a stronger position to take advantage of the weaker. For example, corporations are the primary institutions by which society produces goods and distributes wealth derived from the production of these goods. These institutions are created by law. They're chartered by governments. Their internal structure is sanctioned by governments. Their ability to own property and make contracts is created and enforced by governments. And they're set up to concentrate economic power in the hands of a relatively small number of shareholders and managers, who use this power to exploit workers and appropriate the wealth society creates. In other words, the reason we have to use the government to "redistribute" property is because we have laws that distribute wealth to the rich "before" taxes come into play.

I put "before" in scare quotes here because taxes of course fund institutions like corporate law, contract law, and property law (taxes pay for courts, the police, legislatures, etc.), which distribute wealth continuously. There is no point in time "before" or "after" telling us when any one of these institutions factor into the production or distribution of wealth. While the right would have us believe that "the market" creates wealth, and only *then* does the government collect taxes, in reality corporate law, property law, contract law, and tax law structure markets, and are complimentary parts of a single economic system; they don't exist in a vacuum.

But these laws aren't the only government policies that distribute wealth. Consider what's happened over the past several decades. Nearly all of the income generated from increases in productivity during this period has accrued to the top 10 percent of earners, and the bulk of this increase to the top 1 percent. Since 1989, the top 1 percent has seen its net worth grow by $21 trillion, while the bottom 50 percent has seen its net worth *decrease* by $900 billion.[52] It's not hard to see why. The Federal Reserve used interest rates to tamp down inflation, preventing full employment. We disempowered labor unions. We deregulated the financial industry. We allowed the minimum wage to erode. We entered into trade agreements that allow corporations to offshore jobs. All of these policies distribute income upwards to the most privileged members of society.[53] Combine them with massive tax cuts for the rich and you have a recipe for unprecedented levels of inequality and wild imbalances of economic and political power between the "haves" and the "have nots."

There's a good reason conservatives don't want you to understand this. The rich have been rigging distributive institutions outside of democratic input for hundreds of years, and they want to keep it that way. Conservatives want us to take all of these policies *except for tax law* as a given, believe we're only entitled to what we can acquire in the market, and accept unequal market exchange as natural. However, once we understand how wealth is actually distributed in society, we can see it's arbitrary to single out taxation as "violating property rights" while ignoring other institutions that distribute wealth. Opposition to taxation isn't about protecting property rights, but about keeping a particular set of institutions intact—those that allow the rich to maintain their privilege, entrench their power, and more easily accumulate wealth, while limiting what the rest of society can do to change it.

Meritocracy

The aim of conservatism has always been to justify social hierarchies. These hierarchies are good, according to traditional conservatives, such as Edmund Burke, because they're natural, or even ordained by God. They hold society together in harmony, provide society with order and stability, and thereby prevent society from devolving into anarchy. Conservatives no longer couch arguments for social hierarchies in these terms, for obvious reasons. Americans have always been suspicious of social hierarchies, whether instituted by the church, the state, or concentrated economic power. Instead, conservatives justify modern social hierarchies on the basis of "merit." They claim that in a meritocracy, those who work hard ought to be rewarded for their effort. If I study hard to get into college, earn a degree, compete for a good job, work my way up the corporate ladder, or I start and grow my own business, I should reap the rewards. If social and economic hierarchies arise from this process, no problem. According to conservatives, economic inequality is the "engine of liberty," as it incentivizes individuals to take advantage of their natural talents.[54]

This is a nice story. It would be great if the world actually worked this way. But in reality, the social and economic hierarchies that arise from our so-called meritocracy are arbitrary. While it's true that many people work hard to accumulate wealth and social standing, these hierarchies have much more to do with how we structure our political and economic institutions. The steep rise in income inequality over the last five decades didn't occur because the rich started working harder or became more "meritorious" over this period. It's because they rigged the political and economic system to distribute more wealth to themselves. CEO salaries rose to astronomical levels, for example, because we slashed top marginal income tax rates.[55]

Now consider how some of the wealthiest CEOs earn their income in the first place. In the previous section, we saw how elites have structured our economy over hundreds of years to funnel wealth to a tiny minority of shareholders and managers, for example by enslaving or slaughtering entire peoples, appropriating the commons, using the state to enforce a highly-skewed distributions of wealth, re-interpreting the nature of property rights and contracts to arbitrarily favor commercial enterprises at the expense of workers and communities, corrupting the political system, and so on. There's no reason our economy has to be structured in this manner, and no reason to think that those who are able to accumulate wealth and status within this system do so on the basis of merit.

Take someone like Bill Gates. Gates didn't earn billions of dollars because he worked hard or made important contributions to society. He was successful because he purchased the code for MS-DOS from another programmer, leveraged his social connections to get his operating system on IBM computers, ripped off Apple's graphical user interface, undercut his competition, and exploited network effects to create a monopoly for Microsoft.[56] In other words, Gates acquired his fortune by exploiting a system that rewards ruthless and anticompetitive business tactics.

Nor do other high-level managers accumulate wealth on the basis of merit. One's place within a given corporate-managerial hierarchy often depends on a company's internal politics, personal ambition, one's willingness to throw others under the bus, one's ability to ingratiate themselves with their boss, or just being in the right place at the right time (such as being in charge when the economy is experiencing an economic expansion rather than a contraction).[57] These factors have little to do with merit, yet managers who succeed due to these factors take home hefty paychecks. This is because corporations have the power to hoover up vast sums of wealth and distribute income to those who occupy top positions within these organizations.

Nor are highly-paid professionals who work hard to get through college, pursue graduate degrees, work long hours, and make important contributions to society necessarily compensated on the basis of merit. If someone is able to achieve a high level of professional success in the US, they more than likely had a lot of help along the way. The likelihood of someone attending college, for example, is correlated with parental income.[58] This should come as no surprise. Parents with higher incomes not only have the wherewithal to pay for their children's college tuition, but can provide their children with environments conducive to learning, access to better schools, academic guidance, and resources such as tutors, before they reach college; as well as instill in their children the expectation that they're entitled to resources that will help them get ahead, like asking teachers for extra help or for leeway when turning in school assignments. Some parents can provide their children with social networks that can help them gain admission to elite universities, get an internship or a job interview, or sometimes get hired outright. In other words, even though many children from privileged backgrounds work hard to achieve success, they often owe a great deal of their success to luck.

Not only are those from privileged backgrounds more likely to attend college, but they also enjoy a number of economic advantages once they get to college. The privileged often have the luxury of being able to spend their time in college partying, joining fraternities, and forming social networks with others from similarly privileged backgrounds (which they leverage into job connections after college), whereas those from less privileged backgrounds are more likely to have to spend their college years working part-time jobs, and as a result have little time to form the types of social connections that pay off in the future. Those from privileged backgrounds are also less likely to have to borrow in order to pay for tuition, and are more likely to have parents who can pay their rent, as well as help pay for a down payment on a house later in life. These advantages allow the privileged to accumulate savings and build wealth far more easily than someone who has to pay off a student loan once they graduate, or who doesn't have parents who provide them with tens of thousands of dollars in housing assistance.

These disparities are often amplified by additional factors. Those who achieve financial success, for example, are much more likely to marry someone who also receives a high income. This greatly increases their household income, which in turn allows them to bestow their children with greater advantages. While there's nothing wrong with marrying the person you want, or being able to provide your children with as many opportunities as you can, the benefits you or your children receive as a result have nothing at all to do with merit.

This doesn't mean it's impossible for someone with fewer resources to make it through college or become a highly-paid professional, or that everyone who has achieved professional success in the US was born with a silver spoon in their mouth. Nor does it mean that certain professions shouldn't demand higher incomes than others. But it does show the arbitrary nature of how resources are distributed in our society, and why we should change our institutions if we wish to provide everyone with enough resources to help them live up to their potential.

The idea that some should receive exorbitant salaries because they "work hard" also has problems. It's much easier to work hard if one knows they'll be handsomely compensated, rather than have to toil at a crappy job just to make next month's rent. It's also easier to work hard if one loves their job. While there's nothing wrong with this, it doesn't mean the compensation one receives from working hard is based on merit. And what if you work hard in an industry that's harmful to society? What if you work in the "defense" industry, producing technology that causes death and destruction? What if you work at a cigarette company? What if you work in adjacent industries that exist solely to serve these powerful interests? What if your job, for example, is to figure out ways for corporations to dodge their taxes, skirt regulations, buy off politicians, or spread pro-industry propaganda? Should we consider this type of work meritorious?

This isn't to say that people who make a lot of money, or who work in industries that harm society, are bad people. Most of them are just trying to provide the best life for their families, which is worthy of esteem. The problem isn't with individuals who are trying to provide for their families, but with a system that distributes resources in a highly skewed manner, and rewards those who serve the interests of a small minority of corporations and wealthy elites rather than the interests of society. The fact that some are able to get ahead, make the best of their individual situation, and take care of their families shouldn't provide us with an excuse to ignore injustices that deprive millions of the resources they need to thrive, or preclude us from changing our economic system.

CHAPTER TWO

Classical Liberalism

It's become fashionable for many on the right to refer to themselves as "classical liberals." They want to associate themselves with classical liberal figures, such as John Locke and Adam Smith, along with the ideas they espoused, which are widely associated with the idea of individual liberty. Classical liberals opposed aristocratic privilege, unlimited monarchical authority, and all forms of government tyranny. Modern "classical liberals" on the right claim to carry on this tradition by following the conclusions Locke and Smith drew about the government's role in the economy, namely that its role should be "minimal." According to the right, this allows individuals to keep the fruits of their own labor, as well as engage in voluntary economic exchange with others, both of which are essential for any economic system that aims to promote individual liberty.

The right claims that in order to follow the conclusions of Locke and Smith, we should keep taxes low and government regulation to a minimum. If you work hard at your job to earn income for yourself and your family, you shouldn't have this income taxed away by the government. Likewise, if an employer and an employee want to enter into a "voluntary" employment contract, they should be able to do so without the government interfering, for example by setting a minimum wage. This type of government regulation makes markets less "free." If we want to foster individual liberty, therefore, we should oppose these policies. Instead, we should allow the economy to be guided by the "invisible hand" of the market, which not only allows individuals the freedom to engage in voluntary economic exchange, but will also foster competition, incentivize innovation, and therefore lead to socially beneficial outcomes.

Opposition to taxation and minimum wage laws, however, has nothing to do with individual liberty. Unregulated market economies create wild imbalances of economic power, which gives rise to economic injustice. This happens, for example, when individuals are forced into exploitative economic relationships in order to earn income. When these types of relationships become pervasive in a market economy, cutting taxes for the rich and opposing minimum wage laws only further widens the disparity of power between the exploiter and the exploited; in other words it gives employers greater control over their employees' lives. Conversely, highly progressive levels of taxation and government regulation are among the most effective ways to mitigate this problem—by redistributing income from those with more power to those who might otherwise suffer injustice.

It follows that lower taxes and fewer regulations have nothing to do with letting individuals keep the fruits of their labor. Large imbalances of power between employers and employees allow employers to take home a larger share of what they could in an economy where the balance of power isn't tilted in their favor. When this happens, employers aren't taking home the fruits of their own labor, but the *fruits of their employees' labor*—the literal opposite of what the right claims.

But this is almost beside the point. The wealth our economy generates is largely derived from the resources we inherit from society—the language, the knowledge, the technology, the institutions, and so on. Individuals living today had nothing at all to do with creating this social inheritance. Therefore, only a relatively small share of the wealth we create comes from our labor. If individuals should be entitled to the fruits of their labor, then allowing individuals to keep more than a fraction of the newly-created wealth they help generate should require additional justification, and there's no reason to allow the rich to appropriate the bulk of this wealth for themselves.

It should also become clear that within unregulated market economies, agreements between employers and employees are often far from voluntary. No one voluntarily chooses to be exploited. No one voluntarily accepts wages that barely allow them to feed themselves and put a roof over their head. If they do, it's because they have few other options—hardly a reason to favor "free markets." Nor does anyone voluntarily agree to let the rich keep wealth which is derived from our social inheritance. The only reason these forms of "voluntary" exchange take place is because the "unregulated" market economy—the conditions for which are created and structured by the government, it should be noted—compels them to do so.

In this type of economic system, the idea that the "invisible hand" will magically guide the economy to benefit everyone is a joke. When we lower taxes and cut regulations, we not only further concentrate economic power in the hands of those who already have it—and consequently erode the power of employees, consumers, and communities—but we necessarily concentrate *political* power into the hands of the wealthy, which they use to further rig the system in their own favor and prevent the rest of society from using their government to alter the oppressive economic relationships that come to govern their lives. This is far from the type of system classical liberals like Locke or Smith believed would foster individual liberty.

Individual Liberty

According to the right, when the government taxes me, forcing me to pay for things I don't need or want—for example, social welfare programs—the government violates my individual liberty. If people need things like healthcare, schooling, food, and housing, nobody's stopping them from acquiring these goods in the market. Why does the government need to tax *me* in order to pay for *them*? Everyone should be free to associate with whom they want and acquire the means to provide for themselves and their families, free of coercion by others. A closer look at the economic and political system favored by the right, however, shows it's the right who wants to violate individual liberty, not those who want to give everyone free healthcare.

The first thing to note is *everyone* claims to favor individual liberty. No one goes around saying they hate liberty. When the left advocates programs like Medicare for All, the point is to allow those who need healthcare to be healthy, so they can enjoy the same liberty as those who can afford private health insurance. You can't have liberty if you're dead or broke because you can't afford to pay your medical bills, or because you take on tens of thousands of dollars in debt to pay for treatment.

The same principle applies to society more broadly. You can't enjoy individual liberty if the distribution of property and power in society is such that wealthy elites have most of the say when it comes to important economic and political decisions that may impact your life. What good is individual liberty if you must spend half your waking life taking orders from a boss? If you must work in a dangerous factory or low-paid service industry with little chance of economic mobility, no benefits, wages that pay you barely enough to get by, and bosses who subject you to indignities? If your employer can fire you if you voice your political views? If you face the possibility of financial ruin should you lose your job, become sick or injured, or have to take time off work to care for a loved one? What good are political rights if most of our politicians are beholden to wealthy donors who fund their political campaigns?

In recent decades, economic elites have used a number of tactics to erode individual liberty for ordinary Americans. They've gutted unions, used monetary policy to prevent full employment, entered into trade agreements that allow corporations to offshore jobs, allowed the minimum wage to erode, and so on, thereby diminishing the power of workers. These policies have led to stagnating income while the costs of education, housing, and healthcare have risen dramatically, leading to high levels of poverty and indebtedness, as well as increased economic precarity for much of the middle class. These aren't the conditions traditionally associated with individual liberty.

Classical liberals, such as Thomas Jefferson and Adam Smith, took for granted that individual liberty depended a great deal on *equality*. Jefferson thought America's economy would be based on family farms and self-employed laborers who had the freedom to walk away from any given economic exchange, because they could produce to meet their own needs or demand high wages. When Smith wrote about the benefits of free markets in *The Wealth of Nations*, he described commerce as taking place among small business owners—butchers, brewers, and bakers—not multinational corporations and low-skilled workers who have little power in comparison. In both Jefferson and Smith's ideal economy, wealth would be spread out in a relatively equal manner. They took for granted that individuals wouldn't be dependent on a wealthy minority who owned the bulk of society's resources, or who used their power to restrict the liberty of others.[1] This doesn't mean Jefferson or Smith thought equality between *all* people was desirable, or that institutions that bring about a more equal society for *everyone* are inherently good. Jefferson owned slaves, after all. But for those whose lives they *did* value, equality and individual liberty went hand-in-hand.

One way we might judge whether we're creating the conditions for individual liberty, therefore, would be to see if we're moving towards, or away from, economic equality. We would view the recent trend towards inequality as a red flag, and stop pretending the right's economic agenda promotes individual liberty for anyone other than the rich. The right's agenda has led to stagnating income for poor and middle class Americans over the past several decades, along with a loss of $900 billion of wealth, while the One Percent has seen its wealth increase by *$21 trillion*.[2] This enormous amount of wealth bestows the One Percent with far more liberty than the rest of society could ever dream of possessing. The One Percent doesn't *have* to work. They can easily meet all of their needs, yet still have plenty of money left over even if they were taxed at much higher rates. They can take lavish vacations as often as they want. They can use their money to influence politics and the media. They get to boss around their employees. These are liberties the rest of us don't enjoy. Yet all we hear from the right are complaints about how higher taxes on the rich threaten individual liberty. This is absurd.

Adam Smith would agree. Smith thought that taxation might be a "badge of liberty." If you have substantial property to tax in the first place, you might enjoy enough freedom and independence that you can afford to pay higher taxes without losing your liberty.[3]

Debates about individual liberty don't mean that one side favors individual liberty and the other side opposes it. The right wants the rich to have far more liberty than the rest of society, whereas the left wants the rich to have marginally less liberty, while guaranteeing everyone has enough resources to achieve a *sufficient level of individual liberty*. This requires a much more equal distribution of wealth, and that no one has the power to deny large swaths of the population access to such resources. It's the left that places greater value on individual liberty, not the right.

The Fruits of Labor

The right claims that everyone should be entitled to the "fruits of their labor." If you work hard, take advantage of the opportunities life gives you, and just want to provide for your family, you should be able to do so. Everyone should get to keep what they earn, not have it taxed away by the government. This argument comes from classical liberal philosopher John Locke, who argued that every man "owns" himself and his labor, and therefore owns what he creates when he "mixes" his labor with the earth. I'm a farmer in the seventeenth century. I cut down trees to build my house and plant crops to feed my family. I should get to own my house and keep my food. What could be wrong with that? While this analogy might make sense at first glance, there are a number of problems with the way the right applies Locke's theory to the modern, complex economy we know today.

The first problem is that many on the right act as if allowing individuals to keep the fruits of their labor follows from Locke's theory *as a matter of logic*. I own myself and my labor, "therefore" I should own what I mix my labor with to produce. But the strength of Locke's argument doesn't come from its logic. As libertarian philosopher Robert Nozick pointed out, if I own a can of tomato juice, and pour its contents into the ocean, does this mean I now own the ocean? Of course not.[4] What entitles us to the fruits of our labor is the fact that we value moral principles like fairness, and that we think keeping the fruits of our labor is fair, not the fact that we "own" our labor, or that we "mixed" it with something. Indeed, Locke himself qualified his ideas about property ownership based on his own conception of fairness. He wrote that property acquisition was just only insofar as there was enough left over for everyone else. There's even a fancy name for this, known as the "Lockean Proviso."[5]

There's a good reason those who use the "labor mixing" argument don't want to wade into questions about fairness. This is because they think labor mixing should take place within a market economy, and the way market economies distribute income is often anything but fair. Markets leave much of society without any independent means to provide for themselves. Instead, those without means must depend on labor markets, which are almost always characterized by wide imbalances of power, which allow employers to take advantage of employees. Locke even addressed this issue, writing that, "A man can no more justly make use of another's necessity to force him to become his vassal by withholding that relief God required him to afford to the wants of his brother, than he that has more strength can seize upon a weaker, master him to his obedience, and, with a dagger at his throat, offer him death or slavery."[6]

In today's economy, the degree to which one can force another to become his "vassal" rests on a spectrum. But for millions of workers who must toil in agricultural labor camps, dangerous factories, processing plants, and elsewhere—or in low-paid service industries—the comparison is apt. These workers endure onerous working conditions and are paid barely enough to feed themselves and their families—let alone accumulate savings. Many can expect little hope for long-term economic stability or income mobility. If we want to follow Locke's principles, it makes no sense to rely solely on labor markets to distribute resources.

This doesn't mean Locke thought his principles ought to apply to everyone. After all, he invested in the Atlantic slave trade. His principles didn't extend to slaves, or even wage laborers, who weren't considered full citizens during Locke's time.[7] But we don't have to accept these arbitrary distinctions today. If all individuals should be treated equally, and we're interested in applying Locke's theories to promote individual liberty, we should do everything we can to minimize the likelihood that millions of individuals must submit to the arbitrary will of a moneyed elite.

But there's another problem with the right's argument. Why, for example, should the fruits of my labor encompass the *entirety* of what I mix my labor with to produce, rather than the value my labor *adds* to the product? After all, I didn't create the earth, and therefore have no claim to whatever portion of the product is derived from the earth. Now let's take this principle a step further. In a modern, complex economy, I'm mixing my labor with far more than just the earth. I'm also using the resources I inherit from society—the language, the knowledge, the technology, the infrastructure, the institutions, as well as the labor of others who helped produce the inputs I use to do my job. In other words, market income and the fruits of one's labor aren't the same thing. We all get back more than we contribute individually. Nobel Prize-winning economist Robert Solow estimates that individuals add no more than 12 percent to the value of what they produce; the rest of this value comes from society.[8] To claim everyone is entitled to the "fruits of their labor," then equating the fruits of one's labor with market income, is therefore misleading.

Furthermore, a large portion of income that flows to the wealthiest individuals doesn't come from their labor at all. Most of the increase in economic inequality since the year 2000 is due to the fact that a greater share of income has flowed to capital, and ownership of capital is concentrated in the hands of a wealthy elite.[9] Those who receive income from capital, however, did nothing to earn it. Rather, it's *other* people, along with what we all inherit from society, that generates this wealth. If I own shares in a company, it's the company's *workers* who contribute their labor to the product. Likewise, if I own real estate, the rent I'm able to charge, or the capital gains I receive when I sell my property, is created by my surrounding community. If nearby businesses, jobs, infrastructure, and so on boost demand for my property, then it was the community that made my real estate more valuable while I did nothing.[10]

The right tries to get around this problem by claiming I *did* do something to receive this income—namely that I chose to "invest" my money, rather than waste it on frivolous goods. To the right, the risk one takes to invest their money is a form of sacrifice equivalent to that of labor. But not pissing away money you can afford to lose after meeting your needs involves little sacrifice. It's more akin to a game that only those with enough money can play, those who play are all but guaranteed to win more often than lose, and those with the most wealth have an advantage because they can afford expert advice, along with more opportunities to diversify their assets.[11] This has little to do with earning anything.

Yet another problem for the right's argument is that it's arbitrary to assume that individuals who mix their labor with the earth should own what they produce. Why not assume instead that society can mix its labor *collectively* with the earth, and therefore distribute what it produces as it sees fit, based on the needs of society—especially if society could make better use of the earth than the individuals who happened to first mix their labor with it?[12] This is another reason why we shouldn't rely solely on markets to distribute income. Markets leave vulnerable groups—the elderly, the sick, the disabled, children, and caretakers—without means, allow powerful corporations to despoil the environment, and bestow the wealthiest individuals with the power to corrupt our political system—and rig our economy in a way that ensures income and wealth continue to flow to people like themselves. Society would be better served if we distributed income and wealth in a far more equal manner.

This isn't to say we shouldn't structure the economy in a way that lets the average person keep a great deal of his or her market income. After all, we need a way to distribute resources to individuals if we want them to enjoy economic security, and letting people keep a large portion of their market income can go a long way towards achieving this end. Additionally, letting individuals keep more of their market income incentivizes them to work, which helps grow the economy. All well and good. If we want individuals to keep income that exceeds the amount needed to enjoy economic security or incentivize them to work, however, we should have good reason to do so. The idea that individuals should be entitled to keep the "fruits of their labor" isn't a good reason.

Free Markets

The right claims to favor "free markets." According to the right, the term "free markets" refers to markets that lack coercion—in other words, without the government taxing some people and redistributing their wealth to others. The absence of such coercion leaves individuals free to engage in voluntary exchange when providing goods and services to each other, to the mutual benefit of all transacting parties. This process of exchange, according to the right, is inherently just. We should therefore limit the government's role in distributing society's resources. However, the way the right uses terms like "voluntary," "mutually beneficial," and "coercion" in this context is problematic.

Conservatives use these terms in a circular manner. When they refer to voluntary economic exchange, for example, they mean any exchange that's *agreed upon* by two parties. But the fact that two parties agree to an exchange doesn't make their exchange voluntary in any meaningful sense. When slaves were freed, they were free to enter into "voluntary" contracts with white farmers. "Hey, they agreed to it, must have been voluntary." In reality, freedmen were effectively forced to agree to work under these conditions—which often mirrored slavery. Whites maintained ownership of the land, leaving freedmen little choice but to work under the sharecropping system, a form of indentured servitude.[13] History is rife with similar examples. During the Industrial Revolution, coal companies set up company towns and shipped in workers to remote locales, where they spent 14 hours a day, 6 days a week working in mine shafts, getting black lung, and facing injury or death on the job. Workers often became trapped in these towns, were made to live in company housing, paid in company scrip, and forced to buy their wares at company stores at inflated prices, with literally no way out aside from escaping into the woods. If these workers tried to organize, their employers spied on them, fired them, kicked them out of their houses, had them tossed in jail, and hired Pinkerton goons to beat, intimidate, and sometimes murder them.[14] No one would voluntarily work under these conditions.

But what about today? Aren't workers now much better off? For most of us, yes. For millions of others, not so much. Thousands of immigrants perform backbreaking labor on agricultural labor camps in sweltering heat to provide us with cheap produce. Many others work in dangerous factories, warehouses, and processing plants, or in low-paid service industries serving food, cleaning hotel rooms, working construction, and so on. These workers are paid next to nothing, are often subject to indignities, and can be fired for any reason. If they're an undocumented immigrant, they can be threatened with deportation if they get out of line.[15] These types of jobs may not be as bad as having to work in a mine shaft for 14 hours a day, but the point is that no one would freely agree to work under either set of conditions. Indeed, if this type of exchange can be described as voluntary, then maybe the right should stop complaining that taxation is involuntary. The mere fact that you file your taxes means you "voluntarily" agreed to do so *by definition*, according to the right's logic.

The right might claim it doesn't make sense to compare unfair market exchange with taxation, since it's not the employer's fault if you starve for lack of accepting a job you consider exploitative, whereas with taxation, it's obviously the government's fault if they lock you in jail for not paying your taxes. But this isn't true. The reason someone might starve if they don't work for an employer is because society distributes resources in a way that leaves them without any independent means to provide for themselves, and *enforces this distribution through property law*. This allows employers to control the "means of production," which effectively forces large swaths of the population to work for them.

Alright, back to the point. Calling something "voluntary" does nothing to further your argument if all you mean by voluntary is the fact that two parties came to some agreement. Whether market exchange is voluntary in any relevant sense depends on the degree to which each party can choose to walk away from the exchange if they want. This also happens to be what classical liberals like Adam Smith took for granted. When Smith referred to the "invisible hand" of the market, he assumed economic exchange would take place between self-employed laborers—butchers, brewers, and bakers—who were of equal social standing.[16] Smith wasn't talking about multinational corporations and wage laborers who work on their assembly lines being exposed to disease, or not being able to take bathroom breaks so they can meet their delivery quotas, because they have few other employment options.[17]

Implicit in this conception of voluntary exchange is the idea of *equality*. If you and your employer are on relatively equal bargaining terms, then your employer can't get away with treating you poorly, paying you low wages, and so on. But this isn't the case for millions of workers. While employers can replace low-wage workers with relative ease and generally aren't at risk of folding due to a temporary loss of an individual employee, a worker's only option might be to work for another employer under the same conditions or not be able to pay their bills.

Nor does the fact that economic exchange is "mutually beneficial" justify a given market exchange. If someone agrees to work because they would otherwise starve, and their company pays them *any wage at all*, both parties benefit. But the wages offered by the employer might be so low that the employee can barely afford to feed himself and his family. This is hardly a reason to favor "free markets." This is also funny, because if the fact that an exchange is mutually beneficial justifies the exchange, then any level of taxation, no matter how high, can be justified on these grounds. After all, it's beneficial for you to pay your taxes, since otherwise you can be fined or thrown in jail.

Nor does the fact that taxation involves the use of coercion mean it's a bad thing. We've already seen how taxation might be justified in order to counter forms of market coercion that arise from so-called voluntary or mutually beneficial exchange. But even if the right refuses to accept that certain forms of market exchange are coercive, we've seen that they accept the use of coercion when it comes to something else they value: enforcing property rights. If I come into your house and start eating your food without your permission, you can literally call the cops and have them kidnap me. The right therefore can't use the fact that taxation is backed by the threat of coercion as a reason to oppose taxation. Coercion is baked into market economies, and insofar as coercion is used to enforce property ownership, coercion is good, even according to the right.

Now that we understand that markets inherently involve coercive institutions, and that coercion isn't necessarily bad, we can see that what makes markets free isn't the absence of coercive institutions, but how to structure these institutions to make market exchange just. We can use one form of coercion to enforce things like property rights, while using other forms of coercion to ensure a just distribution of property i.e. one that affords those who engage in market exchange the choice of whether or not to accept a given exchange. This is exactly why we should be taxing the rich and redistributing their wealth. Taxing the rich at high rates would limit their outsized economic and political power over the rest of society. Redistribution also lessens dependence on employers for things like health insurance, or enough income to buy food, pay for school or training, send your kids to daycare, or tide you over if you get laid off. It's therefore the left who favors free markets, not the right.

When the right uses terms like "voluntary exchange" and "mutually beneficial exchange," or "coercion," they're playing word games. They want you to think "voluntary" and "mutually beneficial" mean "good;" therefore we should accept that whatever they describe using these terms is also good. Conversely, they want you to assume "coercion" means "bad;" therefore we should accept that whatever they say is coercive is also bad. But they're only trying to sidestep reasons why policies they favor are bad, and why policies they oppose are good. Similarly, the right uses words like "free" to mask economic and social relationships that are often the opposite of free. They define "free markets" as markets that lack *certain forms* of coercion, while ignoring—indeed promoting—other forms of coercion. In short, the right wants free markets for the rich, and unfree markets for everyone else.

The Invisible Hand

The right believes the economy should be guided by the "invisible hand" of the market. When individuals are left free to act in their own self-interest, competition between economic actors will lead to the proliferation of goods and services, drive down prices, and therefore benefit society—as if guided by an "invisible hand." This idea was famously expounded by classical liberal thinker Adam Smith in *The Wealth of Nations*.[18] Accordingly, the right tells us we should get the government "out" of the market by keeping taxes low and regulation to a minimum. The right, however, has bastardized Smith's idea of the invisible hand.

While Smith assumed markets would play a role in society, he took for granted that laissez-faire economic policies went hand-in-hand with equal access to resources. This allowed individuals freedom *from* markets. The economy Smith envisioned resembled the northern colonies in America during the time he wrote. Families built their own homes, produced their own food and clothing to meet their needs, and only sold goods on the market after these needs were met. Markets played a relatively marginal role in the lives of most Americans, and those who did rely on markets were independent artisans and laborers who could demand high wages, since labor was relatively scarce. A society like this made it plausible that laissez-faire political economy would allow individuals a great deal of freedom. As long as a rough level of equality characterized social and economic relationships, and the state remained at arm's length, individual liberty was unlikely to be threatened.[19]

The fact that these conditions were present in the northern colonies during Smith's time was a historical coincidence, however, not due to some inherent trait of unregulated markets. The US was a vast territory of newly discovered land, rich with natural resources, and open to all—at least if you were white. But these conditions gradually gave way to conditions of scarcity and competition. Land speculators gobbled up the bulk of society's most fertile land, industrialization gave rise to larger business enterprises, and population growth expanded the supply of labor. These developments forced most people to rely on labor markets to survive. They soon found the nature of their work controlled within large, hierarchical organizations, and had to cede control of their daily lives to the will of their employers, who were concerned with making higher profits rather than the workers' well-being.[20] Within these firms arose a strict division of labor, which classical liberals like Smith decried, because it made people "as stupid and ignorant as possible for a human creature to become."[21] In other words, Smith understood that certain market outcomes undermined individual liberty.

The right also misunderstands Smith's concept of self-interest. Smith recognized that when individuals *only* acted in their self-interest, negative outcomes, such as corruption and oligopoly would inevitably follow, writing, "People of the same trade seldom meet together, even for merriment and diversion, but the conversation ends in a conspiracy against the publick, or in some contrivance to raise prices."[22] This is exactly what happened during America's Industrial Revolution. Industrialists like Andrew Carnegie and J.P. Morgan built large monopolies that grew out of control and corrupted every level of government.

Under these circumstances, there's no such thing as Smith's "invisible hand." Instead, corporations and the rich use the government to enact policies favorable to themselves, or prevent policies that run counter to their interests. Corporations bribe Congress to cut taxes for the rich, cut safety regulations, cut environmental regulations, let the minimum wage erode, and enter into trade agreements that give corporations access to cheap labor. They also appoint corporate cronies to enforce labor law and antitrust law, head regulatory agencies, issue judicial rulings favorable to corporations, govern monetary policy to generate unemployment, and so on. These policies distort markets, give power to employers, and destroy the power of workers and consumers.

Nor is there any way to get the government "out" of the market under these conditions. Cutting taxes and regulations gives even more power to those who already enjoy the most influence in society. Economic concentration would remain even after cutting their taxes, allowing those with the most wealth to further corrupt the government. Note this would be true no matter how "small" the government, since according to the right even the most minimal form of government would have to protect property rights—and therefore the distribution of property throughout society—even if this distribution is highly-skewed. Under these conditions, allowing the "invisible hand" to guide the economy only strengthens the hand of concentrated economic power.

The right doesn't advocate minimal government. The primary driver of inequality—and consequently, political corruption—is the existence of large corporations, which are state-sanctioned entities set up to concentrate wealth in the hands of their owners. This was once obvious to traditional conservatives like Christopher Tiedeman, who thought corporations were a "menace to the liberty of the individual," and therefore advocated "the repeal of the statutes which provide for the creation of private corporations."[23] Unless the modern right wants to put their money where their mouth is and abolish this form of government intervention, the right's calls for small government can hardly be taken seriously.

So what choice does this leave us? Since we aren't getting rid of corporations, and we know tax cuts and deregulation only further empower existing concentrations of wealth, we have only one choice—use the government to hold corporations and the rich accountable to the public. Other countries have done this. So did the United States during the New Deal and the Postwar Boom. There's no reason we can't do it again. The right, however, wants do to the opposite. They want to cut taxes and regulations, and pretend the "invisible hand" will magically fix everything, while corporations and the rich accumulate unlimited wealth.

CHAPTER THREE

Constitutionalism

The right professes to believe in "small government." They fear that when the government gets too "big," it can use its power to violate individual rights. The government does this, for example, when it imposes onerous levels of taxation on some segment of the citizenry (the rich), then transfers this wealth to others (the poor) by providing social welfare programs like Obamacare or Social Security. This form of redistribution violates the "property rights" of those who are taxed at higher rates, and allows the government to have greater control over our lives, for example by imposing "death panels" that would give government bureaucrats the power to decide who deserves medial care and who doesn't (this was a lie spread by Republicans during the debate over whether to pass Obamacare into law), or by funding abortions, which the right equates with murder, etc.

In order to limit these forms of government tyranny, according to the right, we should follow the "original intent" of the Constitution. The right claims that the Framers of the Constitution aimed to vest the federal government with only "limited" powers, and made this clear when they produced documents such as *The Federalist Papers*, not to mention the Constitution itself, which lists the government's powers in Article 1, Section 8. The power to establish government programs like Obamacare or Social Security are supposedly nowhere to be found among the enumerated powers. Additionally, the 10th Amendment makes clear that all powers not granted to the federal government are reserved to the individual states. If these states want to establish their own public healthcare systems, no problem. The rights says it just isn't lawful for the federal government to fulfill this role.

While the public may support social welfare programs, this is no reason to violate the Constitution, according to the right. The Framers wished to create *a republic*, not democracy. They feared tyrannical majorities might use the government to violate the rights of minorities, which the right claims is exactly the situation we find ourselves in today. The right agrees with the Framers, and therefore claims we should cut taxes, regulations, and social programs in order to limit the federal government's power, and resist reforms that make our political system more democratic. Cutting taxes and social programs, however, or limiting democracy, has little to do with the limits established by the Constitution.

The Framers didn't intend to create small government. They created the Constitution because they viewed the prior confederation of states as far too weak, and thought the confederation was doomed to collapse. The Framers wished to drastically expand federal authority and create new powers in order to foster commerce and develop the US economy, which they hoped would help the US become a world power. As we'll see, this required placing limits on the power of the *individual states*, not the other way around. Unsurprisingly, opponents of ratification didn't view such powers as "limited." While the Framers did aim to reduce the possibility that democratic majorities might exercise the powers established by the Constitution, to say that the powers themselves are "small" is simply untrue.

There's no reason why the public can't use the powers established by the Constitution to enact reforms favored by majorities. This is especially true given the primary form of tyranny that has come to pervade American society since the time of ratification. The Framers didn't foresee the vast disparity of wealth and power that American capitalism would eventually birth, or that a corporate aristocracy would eventually grow out of control and come to exercise enormous power over the lives of ordinary Americans while using vast sums of wealth to corrupt the government, and keep the government "small" only when it serves their interests. These circumstances demand that majorities enact policies that counter tyranny at the hands of concentrated economic and political power.

Nor should the "original intent" of the Constitution limit majorities from exercising constitutional powers. One reason for this is that there's no such thing as original intent. The Framers, the delegates at the state ratifying conventions, and the general public all held different views on the extent of federal authority established by the Constitution. Figures such as Thomas Jefferson pointed out that the "enumerated powers" doctrine made no sense. The same is true of Antifederalists, who exposed several contradictions that lay at the center of the arguments put forth by the Constitution's proponents. As we'll see, original intent is a made-up concept meant to place arbitrary limits on what the public can use the government to do, in order to protect the interests of the rich.

Furthermore, policies that involve cutting taxes, regulations, and social programs have nothing to do with preserving republican government. These policies concentrate economic and political power into the hands of a plutocracy, which is antithetical to the ideals of republicanism. The right only favors these types of reforms because the right represents the interests of America's plutocracy.

Nor does limiting the power of democratic majorities have anything to do with preventing the government from violating individual rights. Democracies can—and have—aimed to preserve institutional safeguards that protect individual rights. Proponents of democracy want to extend the same rights to *everyone*, and believe these rights are undermined by the right's "small government" policies, which place economic and political power in the hands of a wealthy minority. When the right claims to favor "minority rights," it's only the rights of this minority the right aims to protect.

Small Government

The right claims that the Framers of the Constitution wanted to vest the federal government with only "limited" powers. Making the government "small," we're told, prevents the government from oppressing its citizens. Many on the right therefore claim to be "constitutionalists." They think the government should only be doing things like protecting "property rights," not providing people with healthcare and imposing onerous levels of taxation on others to pay for it. The type of government the right favors, however, is anything but small. Given the enormous disparities in wealth and power that characterize America's economy, a government that only protects property rights allows those with the most wealth to effectively govern the lives of everyone else, often in oppressive ways. A brief look at the history of ratification and some of the developments that followed can shed light on how this came to be.

The Framers didn't wish to limit the federal government to the degree the right claims. They aimed to create a powerful, fiscal-military state that could rival those of their peers—Britain, France, and Spain. In order to do this, the government needed much more power, for example the power to enforce tax collection, build a navy that would protect commercial interests, fund internal improvements such as roads and canals, pay back the nation's creditors, and prevent state governments from being able to manage their own economic affairs. The Framers didn't want states to make commercial treaties with other nations or each other, or be able to tax each other's goods, print money, or enact debtor relief laws. The Framers instead wanted to vest these powers with the federal government, which could administer policy at the national level in a manner more conducive to economic development.[1]

The Framers understood this required a drastic expansion of federal authority. Notes from the Constitutional Convention show that James Madison wanted to render the state governments "subordinately useful," as well as give the national government the "right of coercion" over the state legislatures. He even proposed giving Congress the right to veto any state law.[2]

Because the Constitutional Convention was held behind closed doors, the public wasn't privy to Madison's views. But opponents of ratification didn't view the government's new powers as "limited." They suspected the Constitution's supporters of attempting to establish an aristocracy of bankers, merchants, and large landholders. Some argued the Constitution was "highly dangerous and oligarchic" and was organized so as "to form an aristocratic body." They feared the Constitution would culminate in "a tyrannical aristocracy" ruled by the "wealthy and ambitious, who in every community think they have a right to lord it over their fellow creatures," and would leave the people to "lick the feet of their wellborn masters."[3]

These fears weren't unfounded. Madison thought that allowing the states to inflate away debt with paper money (as well as enact debtor relief laws) was an unjust attack on property, by which he primarily meant the property of creditors.[4] Aristocrats like John Jay also argued that "those who own the country ought to govern it."[5] Likewise, Madison claimed that the Senate "ought to come from, and represent, the wealth of the nation."[6]

Indeed, the type of government the Framers envisioned necessarily required protecting the material interests of the rich. The Framers claimed that in order for the new government to succeed, a "natural aristocracy" of benevolent and "disinterested" statesmen, schooled in the "science" of government—who acted in the public interest—would need to comprise the national legislature. But in order for such an aristocracy to exist, it would have to emerge out of the ranks of the wealthy.[7] The Framers also understood it would only be a matter of time before the bulk of society's resources became appropriated, which would leave little for the majority of the population and lead to conditions that would threaten the property of the wealthy. If the people had the political power to tax away the property of the wealthy, they would do so. In the Framers' minds, it would therefore be necessary to create a form of government that could protect the rich from the majority.[8]

There's a big problem, however, with establishing a government that gives so much power to the rich. Political institutions put in place to achieve these ends might persist whether a "natural aristocracy" emerges or not. When this happens, the powers established by the Constitution allow the rich to veto policies they don't like, with the sole aim of protecting their own wealth and power. Lo and behold, no natural aristocracy emerged after the founding generation. Instead,

America's rapidly developing economy would birth an aristocracy of large corporations and wealthy elites whose sole aim was to enrich themselves. The beginnings of this aristocracy made itself apparent to the French aristocrat Alexis de Tocqueville, who upon visiting the US in the 1830s wrote, "the industrial aristocracy which we see rising before our eyes is one of the most harsh ever to appear on earth." Tocqueville conceded at the time that this aristocracy, "is one of the most restrained and least dangerous," but warned, "this is the direction in which the friends of democracy should constantly fix their anxious gaze; for if ever a permanent inequality of social conditions were to infiltrate the world once again, it is predictable that this is the door by which they would enter."[9]

It turned out Tocqueville's fears were well placed. Businesses would accumulate ever larger sums of wealth, and use this wealth to bribe politicians and enact policies that benefited themselves, while preventing policies that would allow workers and communities to have a voice in their government. After the Civil War, large monopolies grew out of control. Corporations often operated as miniature fiefdoms. They set up company towns, abused their employees, and hired private police forces to intimidate workers who tried to organize. There were hardly any laws that guaranteed collective bargaining rights, limited work hours, or ensured safe workplaces. Large, hierarchical, totalitarian institutions governed the lives of most workers.[10]

Here's where the right's obsession with protecting "property rights" comes in. The right claims that limiting the government to protecting property rights keeps the government "small," thereby limiting oppression. Under the conditions we live, however, a government that "only" protects property rights doesn't do this. Because the distribution of wealth that arises within capitalist economies is so skewed, those who own the most property have the power to govern the lives of everyone else, often under oppressive conditions. Millions of workers toil on labor camps, in dangerous factories, in meat-processing plants, or must work in low-paid service industries with little chance of long-term economic stability or income mobility. While they're at work, if they don't follow their boss' orders, they can be fired, leaving them with the possibility of financial ruin.[11] Those up the chain fare better, but only as a matter of degree. It follows that the degree to which workers might suffer under these conditions depends on the degree to which the distribution of property throughout society is equal, and that "constitutionalism," insofar as it maintains an unequal distribution of property, paves the way for tyranny. This is big government on behalf of the rich.

Now let's go back to what I mentioned earlier. Why is it important that the Constitution vested the government with broad powers? Because we don't have to use these powers to benefit the rich. Constitutional barriers to democracy can be overcome. Organized labor did it during the New Deal era. Civil rights activists did it when they helped end Jim Crow. There's no reason we can't do the same. We could, for example, drastically raise taxes on corporations and the rich, and create a robust welfare state that provides every citizen with the resources needed to live free of control by those with more wealth and power—like healthcare and education. *This* is what the right has a problem with. Opposing popular reforms isn't about whether we favor "big government" or "small government," but whether we favor government that acts on behalf of a wealthy minority, or on behalf of The People.

Original Intent

According to the right, when judges uphold government programs like Obamacare, they ignore the "original intent" of the Constitution—in other words, how the Constitution would have been understood at the time of ratification. The right claims the original intent of the Constitution is evident in the historical record—*The Federalist Papers*, for example—if not in the Constitution itself, and could never have led anyone to believe that the Constitution granted Congress the power to establish programs like Obamacare. But as we'll see, opinion varied among the Framers and the ratifiers, as well as the public, over the extent of federal power granted by the Constitution. In other words there's no single, uniform, original intent of the Constitution.

Not everyone agreed with *The Federalist Papers*. As historian Pauline Maier has pointed out, *The Federalist* wasn't widely published during the debates over ratification, and evidence that *The Federalist* influenced the debates in any state other than New York is sporadic at best. This echoes what James Madison said at the time. According to Madison, *The Federalist* was a partisan document written in order to "promote the ratification of the new Constitution by the State of N. York where it was powerfully opposed, and where its success was deemed of critical importance."[12] Madison elsewhere claimed that the meaning of the Constitution came not from *The Federalist*, but from the state ratifying conventions.[13]

There's a big problem, however, with looking to the state conventions. The delegates at these conventions also disagreed over the extent of federal authority established by the Constitution. Some in the South worried that the Constitution would allow the North to destroy the "property" of the South through taxation or by enlisting slaves to serve in the military.[14] Others assumed the Constitution granted broad authority, but were willing to accept this authority upon ratification, knowing they could amend the Constitution afterwards.[15] Others believed the Constitution granted broad authority, but weren't worried about it because they thought the government would be made up of representatives from the "middling class," whose interests coincided with the public's.[16] Yet others thought the Constitution was "obscure and ambiguous," and therefore weren't sure one way or the other.[17]

These opinions were never reconciled prior to ratification. In some states, delegates wanted to send the Constitution back for revisions, or include amendments that would limit the government beyond what was outlined in the original text. But proponents of ratification believed the Constitution would never be ratified if this were allowed to happen. They thought it would lead to endless debate, and in the meantime the existing confederation of states would collapse.[18] This problem soon became moot, however. Once the first few states ratified the Constitution without amendments, others followed, fearing if they didn't get on board they would be left out of the initial amendment process during the First Congress.[19] Ultimately these delegates voted to ratify the text of the Constitution, not whether the text had a single "meaning," let alone what that meaning was, or whether it would be fixed for eternity.

It might be argued that although the ratifiers never established a single meaning of the Constitution, none of them could have possibly imagined the Constitution could one day allow for something like Obamacare. But this doesn't mean that policies like Obamacare are unconstitutional. It's one thing to say the ratifiers didn't intend to enact specific, unforeseen policies; it's another to say they didn't create the power to do so. The Framers empowered the federal government to "promote the general welfare." During the time of ratification, the range of policy options that served this end may have been limited, but during the two-and-a-half centuries following ratification, a much broader range of possibilities has come into existence. For example, advances in medical technology make it possible to take better care of people and perform new medical procedures. Society's capacity to generate new wealth has likewise grown to a point where we can afford to provide these procedures to all who need them. When the government provides people with healthcare, it's due to economic and technological development, not "activist judges" who ignore the original intent of the Constitution. If the right wants to lament anything, maybe they should lament economic and technological development.

In the meantime, if the right wishes to prevent the government from being able to do things the right doesn't like, they should follow the process outlined in the Constitution. There's nothing stopping the right from organizing support for a constitutional amendment that prohibits the government from providing programs such as Obamacare. Until then, interpreting constitutional authority more narrowly places arbitrary limits on society's ability to govern itself.

Enumerated Powers

According to the right, government programs like Obamacare are unconstitutional. Since the power to establish these programs are not among those specifically enumerated in Article 1, Section 8 of the Constitution, we have no lawful grounds to implement them. In case this isn't obvious, the 10th Amendment makes clear that all powers not delegated to the federal government are reserved to the states. But is Congress really limited to the enumerated powers?

Not according to Thomas Jefferson. When Pennsylvania congressman James Wilson argued during the ratification debates that Congress would be limited to the enumerated powers, Jefferson explained that Wilson was wrong. In a letter to James Madison, Jefferson claimed this was obvious to anyone who simply read the Constitution. Jefferson reasoned that the Articles of Confederation, under which the previous national government had been established, contained language that limited the federal government to powers that were "expressly delegated," but that this language was absent from the Constitution.[20]

There's evidence to support Jefferson's argument. Records of the Constitutional Convention show the decision to omit the phrase "expressly delegated" was deliberate. Some of the Framers argued that to place such a limit on the new government would have been "destructive to the Union."[21] Others observed that the Constitution listed things Congress *couldn't* do in Article 1, Section 9 (for example, grant titles of nobility). If Congress was limited to powers that were specifically enumerated, why would the Framers need to list things Congress couldn't do, unless there were *implied* powers beyond those enumerated?[22]

Thankfully the Supreme Court has often ignored the enumerated powers doctrine, or at least stretched the meaning of the powers that *are* enumerated so broadly that it hardly matters. Conservatives might claim this is an abuse of power, but it's in line with what the Framers intended, as well as what many of the ratifiers, along with much of the public, assumed.[23]

What about the 10th Amendment? The right points out that the 10th Amendment makes clear that all powers not given to the federal government are reserved to the states. The right thinks this supports the idea that Congress is limited to the enumerated powers. But it doesn't. The fact that various powers are divided between the state and federal government isn't the issue. Rather the issue is *which* powers the state and federal governments possess. The 10th Amendment says nothing about this. That's why Antifederalists tried to get the "expressly delegated" language included in the 10th Amendment. However, they were rejected for the same reason the language was omitted from the original document. James Madison explained, "It was impossible to confine a Government to the exercise of express powers; there must necessarily be admitted powers by implication, unless the Constitution descended to recount every minutia."[24] In other words, the 10th Amendment does nothing. Indeed, one might wonder why the 10th Amendment even exists.

Federalists supported the 10th Amendment as a political tactic. They thought the entire Bill of rights unnecessary, including its watered-down 10th Amendment. But they supported the Bill of Rights in order to undercut their opponents. If the Antifederalists had their way, there might have been another constitutional convention. Federalists wanted to stave off this possibility, which would have destroyed everything they'd been working for. Passing the Bill of Rights was a way for Federalists to avoid this scenario by making it look as if they were compromising with their opponents, while at the same time leaving, as Alexander Hamilton would later explain, "the structure of the government and the mass and distribution of its powers where they were."[25] Antifederalists understood this perfectly. When it became evident that the Bill of Rights wouldn't change anything, they argued it was "good for nothing," and was "calculated merely to amuse, or rather to deceive." The Antifederalists were at the mercy of their opponents, however. When Antifederalists opposed the Bill of Rights, Federalists accused them of being unreasonable, since the Bill of Rights was the Antifederalists' idea to begin with![26] The Federalists therefore outplayed their Antifederalist opponents, helped pass the Bill of Rights, and avoided having to tear up the Constitution and start over.

A Republic, Not a Democracy

When Republican presidential candidate Donald Trump won the Electoral College in 2016 without winning the popular vote, Democratic voters complained that the Electoral College is undemocratic. Likewise, when Senate Republicans—which represent about 40 million less people than Senate Democrats—block popular legislation, we hear similar complaints about the undemocratic nature of the Senate. The right dismisses these complaints, claiming democracy is little more than "mob rule," under which the majority will inevitably violate the rights of minorities. The right therefore loves to point out that the Framers of the Constitution didn't want to create a democracy, but instead wanted to create *a republic*. The distinction the right draws between a republic and a democracy, however, is misleading.

A republic and a democracy aren't mutually exclusive concepts. When we passed a constitutional amendment to allow the direct election of senators, or passed an amendment to allow women to vote, or abolished Jim Crow laws, the US became more democratic, but it didn't cease to be a republic. The same would be true if we took even greater steps in this direction. The defining characteristic of republican government is the fact that it's not a monarchy. This leaves a wide range of possibilities, which can lean towards democracy, or towards what the right wants—an aristocracy (more specifically a *plutocracy*).

Institutions like the Electoral College and equal state representation in the Senate have nothing to do with republican government. Indeed, opponents of ratification claimed these institutions were antithetical to republican government. Antifederalist author "A Columbian Patriot" argued that the Electoral College was "nearly tantamount to the exclusion of the voice of the people in the choice of their first magistrate. It is vesting the choice solely in an aristocratic junto, who may easily combine in each state to place at the head of the union the most convenient instrument for despotic sway."[27] At the Constitutional Convention, New York Delegate Melancton Smith argued that unless senators were barred from serving more than six years in any twelve, the Senate would be "inconsistent with the established principles of Republicanism."[28]

These institutions were the outcome of back room deals meant to gain support for ratification. The Electoral College was created as a way to get buy-in from slave states during the Constitutional Convention. It would give these states a disproportionate amount of power by counting their slaves towards their apportionment of delegates when choosing the President.[29] Equal representation in the Senate was a ploy by some delegates at the Convention to ensure that their (less populous) states would maintain some level of parity with larger states in the new government.[30] These institutions weren't created on the basis of establishing a republican form of government, but the result of political haggling.

Why does the right support institutions like the Electoral College and equal representation in the Senate? Because it benefits the Republican Party, under which the right has consolidated its political power. The Electoral College favors less populous, Republican-leaning states, since the number of electoral votes apportioned to each state include one for each senator, which number the same for each state regardless of the size of each state's population. Equal representation in the Senate gives states like Wyoming, which has a population of 585,501, the same amount of representation as California, which has a population of 39,250,000. Because most of these less-populous states lean to the right on political and economic issues, institutions such as the Electoral College and the Senate provide concentrated economic power with a firewall against more populous states that lean to the left.

The right's use of these tactics fits a broader pattern. The right uses any institution they can in order to block reforms that run counter to their own interests, no matter the original purpose of such institutions, or the principles these institutions were meant to serve. The Senate filibuster wasn't intended as a tool to kill all legislation that doesn't meet a 60-vote threshold in the Senate. This practice only became normalized—gradually—over the past 50 years, which Republicans use to thwart any legislation that might hamper corporate profits.[31]

Republicans have also been utterly shameless when it comes to exploiting the congressional redistricting process. Leading up to the 2010 midterm elections, Republicans launched Operation Ratfuck, pouring hundreds of millions of dollars into state-level congressional races in order to flip Democratic legislative majorities or maintain Republican majorities, in order to control the redistricting process that coincided with the US Census (taken every 10 years).[32] And it worked. Republican-controlled state legislatures gerrymandered their states' districts to favor Republican candidates, resulting in an average of 16-17 extra Republican seats in the House of Representatives over the next decade.[33]

The same is true when it comes to voting rights. Republicans have supported a variety of voter suppression tactics, including voter ID laws, voter roll purges, voter caging, felon disenfranchisement laws, limiting same-day registration, limiting polling places in Democratic voting districts, reducing early voting, empowering state officials to challenge mail-in ballots, and voter intimidation—all of which disadvantage the right's political opponents.[34]

Likewise, the right has packed every level of the judiciary with young, incompetent, free market ideologues who aim to ensure that no matter what the public wants, if these policies run counter to the interests of corporations and the rich, they're more likely to be overturned—and that the right's power to overturn such legislation will persist decades into the future. In 2016, Republican Senate Majority Leader Mitch McConnell refused to confirm Supreme Court nominee Merrick Garland, appointed by then-President Barrack Obama, effectively packing the Court.[35]

More recently, the Republican Party attempted to steal the 2020 presidential election. When so-called republican institutions (in this case the Electoral College) failed to deliver the election to Republican President Donald Trump, the Party tried to invalidate the election results based on unsubstantiated claims of voter fraud.[36] Republicans don't do these things on the basis of defending "republican" government, but to boost their chances of winning elections, maintain their outsized grip on our political system, and enact policies that serve the rich.

Nor does the right care about minority rights. The most vulnerable minorities in the US are undocumented immigrants, Muslims, the poor, LGBTQ individuals, left-wing political dissidents, and whistle-blowers—groups whose rights the right has historically cared little about protecting, and routinely aims to violate. They want to deny citizenship to immigrants, place Muslims under FBI surveillance, deny equal funding for schools in poor neighborhoods, allow businesses to discriminate against the LGBTQ community, lock left-wing protesters in jail, and try whistle-blowers under the Espionage Act.[37] This pattern makes clear that the right only wishes to protect one minority—the rich.

Tyranny of the Majority

The right views democracy as "tyranny of the majority." According to this argument, if everyone has equal political power, majorities can easily trample the rights of "the minority." Ben Shapiro is explicit about which minority the right is referring to, pointing out that, "The majority, which has since time immemorial wanted to rob the richer minority, moved to rewrite the system to allow such wealth confiscation. They did it under the guise of fairness. But once the process is overthrown, the tyranny of the majority is no longer speculative: it is a living, breathing reality."[38] The "richer minority" indeed. The right therefore scoffs at the idea that our political system should be more democratic. But democracy isn't tyranny of the majority at all.

There's nothing that precludes a democracy from establishing institutional safeguards against tyranny. When individuals advocate for more democracy, this doesn't mean they want to abolish the Bill of Rights. They just want everyone to have an equal say in our political system. This *requires* the maintenance of equal rights. Once individuals lose their rights, their political power is necessarily diminished, and the polity ceases to be democratic. The principle of protecting individual rights is therefore baked into the idea of democracy. This doesn't mean a majority within a democracy can't violate this principle and remove legal safeguards meant to protect minorities. But the same is true of any political system. The right, for example, favors a form of government that they claim more closely resembles what the Founding Fathers originally set up. But this form of government carried out genocide against America's indigenous inhabitants, allowed slavery for the first 89 years of its existence, allowed another 100 years of Jim Crow, and to this day promotes wild imbalances of economic and political power that undermine the rights of vast swaths of the population.

There's good reason the right focuses their criticism solely on the flaws of democratic government. Under the right's preferred form of government, millions of Americans lack enough economic and political power to exercise their rights in any meaningful way. My right to vote, for example, doesn't mean much if I can only vote for candidates who are pre-selected for me by a corporate elite, and my political views won't affect policy even if "my" candidate wins. Nor does freedom of speech mean much if that speech can be drowned out by those with more wealth, who spend billions of dollars funding think tanks, academic departments at universities, and public relations campaigns, to spread their ideas through a vast network of corporate media. Indeed, what good are any rights if, for most of their waking lives, large swaths of the population must work at jobs they despise under the control of superiors who boss them around, monitor their every move, often limit their political speech, and wear them out to the point that even when they aren't at work, they lack the time and energy needed to meaningfully participate in their community?

The right sees nothing wrong with this. They openly claim that money is "speech;" therefore, campaign spending shouldn't be regulated. They say "property rights" are absolute; therefore, taxation and wealth redistribution are illegitimate. And if you don't like having to take orders from your boss, they suggest you should just find another job, never mind that those who face the most onerous working conditions have few other options, which is why they had a job that limits their freedom in the first place. In other words, the right favors the formal recognition of rights, but ignores how imbalances of power in society undermine those rights in practice.

The right's preferred form of government is a cheap, imitation version of what proponents of democracy strive to achieve in substance, which is for individuals to have control over their lives, as well as an equal say in the political and economic decisions that affect them. Reforms that bring about these ends aren't tyranny, but go hand-in-hand with liberty. If the distribution of wealth and political power in society is skewed to ensure freedom for only a wealthy minority, while undermining the rights of others, then policies that equalize economic power—for example, progressive taxation—limit the power of the rich to rule our lives. They act as a safeguard against tyranny of the minority.

CHAPTER FOUR

Capitalism

The right claims that capitalism offers the most freedom of any economic system. If we want as many people to have as much freedom as possible, we need to have a developed economy that provides us with high living standards. But according to the right, the only way this can happen in the long run is for countries to adopt capitalism and "free trade." Developing countries, for example, can accumulate wealth by opening their economies to global capital, exporting raw materials, providing foreign corporations with access to cheap labor, and importing finished goods. These countries shouldn't impose tariff subsidies, enact capital controls, or implement expansive welfare states, high taxes, and onerous regulations, all of which supposedly hamper market efficiency. Developed countries should likewise refrain from adopting policies that hamper free markets, or we'll find ourselves regressing down a slippery slope to "socialism," which inevitably ends with mass starvation and totalitarian dictatorships—just see the USSR under Stalin and China under Mao—or even fascism, which the right claims is a left-wing phenomenon. Venezuela offers a more contemporary example, where "socialist" policies have supposedly led to widespread food shortages, forcing some people to eat rats and dogs in order to survive.

The right also points to technological innovation as a reason to support free markets and forego left-wing economic reforms. We're told that capitalism is solely responsible for most of the technological innovation that allows us to enjoy high living standards today. If we want living standards to continue to rise, we shouldn't adopt left-wing policies, because these policies waste wealth that could otherwise be used to invest in new technology.

Furthermore, while some problems have occurred under capitalism—like monopolies, environmental destruction, and war—these problems aren't the fault of capitalism, but of government "intervention" in the economy. Monopolies, for example, are created when corrupt politicians regulate industry on behalf of incumbent firms. If we want to eliminate these problems, according to the right, we just have to move further in the direction of capitalism, meaning we should eliminate the government's authority to regulate corporations, and allow the market to foster competition between businesses, which will lead to the most socially-beneficial outcomes.

The right makes these arguments to trick society into making a false choice—between "capitalism" and "socialism"—even though countries have a wide variety of options available to them. What the right really means is that we should force certain policies—those that primarily benefit corporations and their investors—on domestic populations, rather than allow ordinary people to have a say in how their economies are organized. Take "free trade." No country has ever joined the ranks of the developed world by following "free trade" policies—including the US, which only pushed for free trade once it became advantageous for them to do so. It turns out that countries develop faster, wealth is more widely shared, and the poor fare much better when nations are free to develop independently, often by adopting policies that run counter to free trade. Indeed, free trade is a misnomer, since free trade policies are imposed by foreign lending institutions and corrupt local elites who repress their citizens, often with military aid from developed countries at the behest of capitalists in those countries who profit from unequal trade partnerships; and much of the "trade" that occurs under free trade regimes doesn't take place between trade partners at all, but is internal to large, multinational corporations who simply want to move some of their operations across nearby borders so they can take advantage of lower labor costs, lower taxes, and lax regulation.

Nor do left-wing economic policies lead to mass starvation and totalitarian dictatorships. Left-wing reforms have expanded freedom for millions of people, most notably in the Nordic countries, which have less poverty, offer more economic mobility, and compare favorably to the US in a number of other economic indicators. And while the right points to atrocities committed by Stalin and Mao in order to discredit alternatives to the right's preferred policies, the right ignores similar atrocities committed by capitalist governments in India, Latin America, China, Africa, and Southeast Asia. This is understandable, given that the victims of these atrocities number well over 100 million.

Nor is Fascism left-wing. Fascists allied with capitalists to gain political support, and once in power, bolstered the power of capitalists while doing everything they could to destroy the left. To invert this reality, the right uses a host of fallacious arguments to confuse their audience.

The claim that Venezuela shows what happens when we adopt "socialist" economic policies is also problematic. Venezuela's economy is capitalist, not socialist, a fact that some on the right were happy to tout when Venezuela's economy was booming under President Hugo Chávez. Venezuela's subsequent economic failures weren't due to socialist policies, but the result of economic missteps that countries that are more "socialist" have avoided, along with economic sanctions by the US. Indeed, Venezuela's economic story says more about the power of capitalism—when wielded by the most powerful government in the world—to destroy weaker nations that eschew capitalist orthodoxy, than it does about left-wing economic reforms.

We'll also see that, far from leading to technological advancement, when capitalism is allowed to grow unchecked, capitalist firms do everything in their power to stifle innovation, erasing many of the benefits capitalist ideologues tout to justify their opposition to left-wing economic reforms. Nor is capitalism sufficient in order to develop advanced technology. The most important technological advances we've seen (computers and other advanced electronics, the Internet, and so on) have relied heavily on government funding for their existence. This undercuts the claim that we need to slash taxes and regulations if we hope to benefit from new technology.

And while the right tries to absolve capitalism of responsibility for the wreckage it's caused by claiming that actually-existing capitalism is not really capitalism, but "crony capitalism," I'll show that oligopoly, corruption, and unchecked economic inequality are intrinsic features of capitalism.

Free Trade

There's widespread agreement among the political establishment—as well as the economics profession—that for countries to develop, they need to adopt "free trade." According to proponents of this doctrine, the free flow of capital both within and across national borders will lead to its most efficient use, allowing developing countries to specialize in producing things they're good at, like agricultural exports and raw materials. This allows these countries to accumulate wealth, and invest this wealth to further develop their economies over time, as well as purchase finished goods from developed countries. Accordingly, governments shouldn't impose tariffs or offer other subsidies to businesses, nor restrict the movement of capital; they should keep inflation low, reduce government bureaucracy, maintain the value of their currencies, and keep social spending low in order to pay off creditors. These policies have lifted millions of people out of poverty, according to proponents of free trade, and indeed are the only way impoverished countries can develop in the long run.

Proponents of free trade, however, couldn't be more wrong. No country has ever joined the ranks of the developed world by adopting "free trade." Britain developed its economy by stealing resources from its colonies—like slave-picked cotton—to fuel its textile industry, banning exports from its colonies that competed with its own products, and by using tariffs to protect its manufacturing sector from superior products made elsewhere.[1] Similarly, the US developed its economy by stealing land from its indigenous inhabitants, relying on its slave economy to bolster other industries (such as shipping), using the profits from cotton production to fuel investment in other industries, using tariffs to protect infant industries, giving away free land to American settlers, and by using the government to subsidize transportation infrastructure and protect American industry from superior British goods.[2]

These weren't the only factors that allowed countries like Britain and the US to develop. Deforestation in Europe, along with the presence of large coal deposits in England, led to a shift to alternate forms of energy, and subsequently a shift to new technologies that would fuel industrialization. Competition among European states during the eighteenth century developed these states' fiscal, bureaucratic, and military capacities, which they used to dominate and pillage poorer countries. None of these factors have anything to do with free trade.[3]

If we want to see how free trade actually works, we can look at other countries during this time that adopted free trade. When Britain was siphoning off wealth from its colonies and using tariffs to protect its early textile industry in order to develop, China had free trade. Its markets were highly integrated, extended over a large area, and encompassed a vast supply of natural resources. Serfdom had largely disappeared by this time, whereas it still persisted in Europe. Labor mobility was much greater than in Britain. And taxes and public debt were far lower than they were throughout Europe. Yet China failed to industrialize.[4] Or take Egypt. Whereas the American colonies won their independence from Britain, and pursued an independent development path using the policies listed above, Egypt was precluded from adopting similar policies by Britain, France, and their Ottoman proxies. Despite having the capacity to develop a modern manufacturing base, a large labor force, as well as its own cotton industry, Egypt failed to develop because capitalist powers like Britain and France didn't want to face industrial competition from Egypt and wanted access to Egyptian markets and raw materials.[5]

It was only after using protectionist policies—along with slavery, conquest, and theft—to establish a "comparative advantage" over underdeveloped countries that Britain and the US adopted "free trade" policies and started recommending that developing countries do so as well. It doesn't take a genius to figure out why. The US and Britain wanted new markets to sell manufactured goods, along with access to the cheap imports, cheap labor, and raw materials that developing countries could provide them. The US and Britain didn't recommend these countries adopt free trade because they believed it would help these countries develop, but because it benefited the US and Britain.

Now take Russia. Russia turned itself from a backwards peasant society into one of the world's two major industrial super powers in just a few decades using central planning, and did so despite enduring military attacks from the US, a major civil war, and two world wars that destroyed much of the country and killed tens of millions of its citizens. In contrast, Brazil, which was comparable to Russia in size, started at roughly the same level of economic development, had access to an enormous stock of natural resources, and had no enemies attacking it, stuck with free trade policies during this period. Yet Brazil remained an economic backwater.[6]

This isn't to say that countries should adopt Soviet-style central planning or admire dictators like Joseph Stalin. But what does the comparison between Russia and Brazil say about free markets and free trade, under which millions of Brazilian peasants fared worse than their Russian counterparts? Nor could central planning sustain the Russian economy indefinitely, but the degree of central planning carried out by the Soviet Union is far from the only alternative to the brand of free markets and free trade promoted by capitalist powers like the US and Britain. Indeed, the market reforms that followed the collapse of the Soviet Union only further hampered Russia's economic development, pushed *72 million people* into poverty, created a drug epidemic, doubled Russia's suicide rate, increased violent crime by a factor of four, and likely killed several million people.[7]

The right eschews comparisons like these, instead comparing countries that share only superficial similarities. In order to tout the merits of free trade, the right points to North Korea and South Korea. After the Korean War, South Korea's capitalist economy developed, whereas North Korea's communist economy became one of the most dysfunctional in the world, and remains so to this day. There's a problem with this comparison, however. North Korea was literally flattened by the US during the Korean War, had fifteen percent of its population slaughtered, then succumbed to authoritarian rule, led by despots who chose economic isolation and military spending in order to deter further US aggression rather than develop its economy. Again, these aren't the only available alternatives to free trade and free markets.

To see one of these alternatives, we can look to South Korea itself. After the Korean War, South Korea's economy was less "free" than India's, yet South Korea developed faster. As social theorist Vivek Chibber shows, both South Korea and India relied heavily on state intervention to regulate private industry. South Korea, however, achieved a higher rate of development because its state apparatus was stronger, and because the state used its power to discipline its capitalist class, forcing investment into key sectors. India's state capacity was weaker in comparison, leaving key investment decisions in the hands of capitalists. This suggests that economic development depends not on how "free" a nation's markets are, but on the nature and extent of state economic intervention.[8]

Some on the right try to get around this problem by claiming that India's economy was socialist during this period. Conservative writer Kevin Williamson argues that because Indian Prime Minister Jawarahal Nehru shared socialist economic views with Ghandi, and because the Indian government instituted various five-year plans to develop the Indian economy—supposedly just like the Soviet Union—then India must have also been socialist.[9] At no point in history, however, has India had a socialist economy. Prior to independence, India had been under British rule for nearly a century. Its economy was capitalist. The means of production were privately-owned. When India won its independence, its government aimed to implement a version of socialism, but this doesn't mean India actually became socialist. Private ownership remained the norm, and India's "five-year plans" shared few similarities with those implemented by the Soviet Union. In the Soviet Union, the government directly controlled the country's factories, and could therefore direct production and distribution in order to adhere to its plans. The Indian government, however, lacked the power to implement its economic agenda. Instead, India's capitalist class ran India's economy.[10]

Williamson also compares India to capitalist Taiwan and Hong Kong. But Taiwan and Hong Kong also adopted a high degree of state intervention. Taiwan embraced friendlier policies towards foreign investors, but also used state-owned enterprises more extensively. Singapore lured capital investment with subsidies; invested in infrastructure, education, and key industries; owns all of the land in the country; and supplies 85 percent of all housing. Hong Kong is the exception, but its economy can hardly be considered an example of free trade, as all its land is owned by the government.[11]

This pattern holds true generally. Since the end of World War II, developing countries have seen their economies grow faster when choosing not to follow "free trade" policies. In the 1960s and 1970s, per capita income grew by 3 percent annually in these economies, much faster than they did during the age of imperialism and free trade. These countries relied on state-owned enterprises, implemented capital controls, invested in public healthcare and education, enacted land reform, nationalized key resources, and used their governments to coordinate investment in key industries. Incomes in these countries subsequently grew, poverty rates fell, and the gap between rich and poor countries began to close.[12]

From the 1980s to 2000, however, many of these countries were forced to adopt free trade. They faced balance of payments crises brought on by a global recession in the early 1980s. To dig themselves out, they turned to the International Monetary Fund and the World Bank for loans, which required them to make their central banks more "independent" (in other words, less accountable to elected governments), allow capital to flow in and out of their economies, privatize key industries, deregulate labor markets, and cut government spending on pensions, healthcare, and public sector jobs. These countries subsequently saw their economies grow at a slower rate—about half as fast as they grew during the prior two decades—and economic inequality significantly worsened.[13]

This trend was only reversed once western influence began to wane. When Argentina faced a financial crisis and defaulted on its debt in 2001, its economy contracted by 11 percent, unemployment rose to 22 percent, and the poverty rate rose to 57 percent. In order to escape this crisis, the government eschewed "free trade" by devaluing its currency, and increased domestic consumption and investment. Argentina's economy then grew by 63 percent and poverty was reduced by nearly two-thirds.[14] A number of left-wing governments were elected to office in Latin America during this time—in Argentina, Brazil, Bolivia, Ecuador, Chile, Uruguay, Paraguay, El Salvador, Nicaragua, and Honduras—after which growth improved in the region, and poverty declined dramatically.[15]

This pattern can also be seen within developed economies. From the end of World War II to the early 1970s, the US economy saw its fastest rate of growth, and the economic gains from this growth were widely shared. The US also suffered no financial crises. Yet this was a period during which tax rates were much higher—with marginal rates as high as 91 percent on top earners—a much higher percentage of the workforce was unionized, the banking system was tightly regulated, and the federal minimum wage grew to over $12 an hour (adjusted for inflation). Over the past five decades, however, we've seen unionization rates fall dramatically, along with wave after wave of financial deregulation, privatization, trade agreements, offshoring, tax cuts for the rich, and so on, with growth falling substantially during this period, coupled with multiple financial crises.[16]

The global financial crisis that began in 2007 offers another example of what happens when governments follow the advice of free trade ideologues. In the wake of the crisis, the European Union's member states were forced to undergo fiscal austerity. These states couldn't devalue their currency because they were tied to the Euro, and they couldn't undergo monetary expansion because they were at the mercy of the European Central Bank. Blame was cast at the supposed profligate spending of states like Greece and Spain, but when these countries slashed their budgets, this only worsened the crisis.[17] In contrast, the US didn't introduce market discipline to the same extent. Instead, the Federal Reserve pumped trillions of dollars into the economy, and the government enacted a modest economic stimulus package and ran massive budget deficits, which allowed the US to recover faster than Europe.[18]

Nor has free trade delivered on its promise to alleviate global poverty. In 2015, the UN published its final report of the Millennium Development Goals, which claimed that global poverty had been cut in half since 1990. Free trade ideologues tout this statistic as evidence showing free trade works. The UN report, however, doesn't show this at all. For one, most of the reduction in global poverty during this period occurred in China, which didn't develop using free trade policies. China is dominated by state-owned enterprises, and the state controls most of the banking system.[19] It was also able to attract foreign investment because it had a large, educated workforce that had been created under communism. Second, the UN's statistics underestimate the number living in poverty. The UN sets the cutoff for living in poverty at $1.90 per day. But the consensus among scholars is that the cutoff should be much higher—some say as high as $12.50. Proponents of free trade use $1.90 per day because it fits the narrative that their economic recommendations have reduced poverty. When using higher numbers, a much different story emerges. If we use a $4 per day threshold, for example, and exclude China, poverty has barely budged.[20]

Using income as the sole metric to measure the success of free trade policies is also problematic. When incomes rise, this doesn't necessarily mean that the lives of those who receive this income have improved. This is because free trade often deprives people of other means by which they may provide for themselves. Much of the global population doesn't depend solely on income to meet their needs, but can instead subsist on their own by living off the land and relying on their communities to distribute resources where they're needed. They might earn income to supplement these needs, but they're not wholly dependent on labor markets to survive. Free trade, however, often forces these people off their land. When large, multinational corporations enter their communities, these corporations cause pollution, destroying water sources and crops. The corporations are also subsidized by their home governments, which enables them to flood foreign markets with cheap goods, undercut smaller competitors, and put them out of business. In other cases peasants are literally forced off their land by private goon squads who beat, intimidate, or murder those who resist. Once this happens, peasants are forced into labor markets and either have to work in sweatshops for below-subsistence wages, or migrate elsewhere in search of a better life.[21]

It would be naive to assume "free trade" is anything other than a continuation of five centuries of colonial pillage. But the evidence shows this to be true. Free trade is a euphemism given to policies that allow investors in rich countries to continue to extract wealth from developing countries, driving inequality both within and between countries, and creating widespread misery.

Stalin and Mao

The right claims we shouldn't implement social-democratic welfare programs in the US because this is "socialism," and socialism has led to mass starvation under totalitarian dictatorships. Libertarian thinker Matte Kibbe warns, "Let me name a few names: Vladimir Lenin and Joseph Stalin; 67 million people dead. Mao Zedong, the greatest Chinese experiment in socialism, killed anywhere from 38 to 45 million depending on the estimate."[22] Even though the Soviet Union enjoyed high rates of growth as its economy developed, and China greatly reduced poverty and improved public health and education under communism, these achievements came at too great a cost. Any move towards "socialism" will eventually either run up against problems with distributing resources like food, or succumb to totalitarianism, ending in widespread human suffering, according to the right. There's no causal relationship, however, between social-democratic welfare programs and mass starvation or totalitarianism.

Countries that have implemented social-democratic welfare programs remain among the freest and most prosperous in the world. Many rank ahead of the US in a number of indicators of well-being, such as happiness, press freedom, and lack of political corruption.[23] Even by the right's standards, some of these countries compare favorably to the US—for example, in the rate of start-up companies and "economic freedom" (as defined by the right-wing Heritage Foundation).[24] It's also without question that those at the bottom of the economic ladder in these countries enjoy far greater levels of freedom than their counterparts in the US.[25] Indeed, if the types of social-democratic welfare programs we find in other wealthy countries were implemented in the US, they would supplement a wide array of successful programs, like Social Security and Medicare, which have not only drastically reduced poverty but remain widely popular.

But if the right wants to judge socialism (and by extension social-democratic welfare states) solely by the atrocities perpetrated by regimes the right considers socialist, then it's only fair to judge "capitalism" by the same standards. When we do this, we see that the death and destruction wrought by "capitalism" far surpasses that of "socialism." In the United States, white settlers, along with the US Army, slaughtered hundreds of thousands of Native Americans, spread disease among the Native American population, and stole their land. In Ireland, English landowners—despite having enough food to feed the local population—exported their crops to global markets in order to accumulate wealth, killing a million people during the Irish Potato Famine.[26] In the West's colonies during the El Niño famines of the late nineteenth century, food sat around awaiting export while much of the local population starved. Between 30 and 60 million people in India, China, Brazil, and elsewhere perished under famines caused by their colonial rulers. Author Mike Davis describes these episodes as "late Victorian holocausts."[27] Capitalism killed millions more in colonial Africa, most notably in the Belgian Congo beginning with the rule of King Leopold II. Corporations spawned from capitalist economies ravaged the Congo to harvest ivory and rubber. They shared their profits with Leopold's Congo Free State, and worked side-by-side with the State to enslave, murder, and spread disease among the local population.[28]

Capitalism killed *tens of millions* more in India. We can see this by comparing India with China from 1947-1980. As China and India each transitioned to independence in the late 1940s, both countries started at roughly the same level of development and had nearly identical mortality rates. China adopted a more "socialist" program, providing basic health care, food, and education to its population, whereas India adopted a more "capitalist" program, limiting public food distribution to urban areas in normal times and to rural areas only during famines. This helped India avoid high death tolls during famines, but India's excess mortality rate was on average 4 million per year greater than China's during this time span, even when we include the Chinese Famine. In other words, the death toll from leaving food distribution to the market during this period was on the order of 100 million, more than the number of deaths than can be attributed to Stalin and Mao combined.[29]

This should come as no surprise. Hundreds of thousands of Americans, if not millions, are painfully familiar with the devastation caused by relying on markets to distribute vital resources. Despite being the wealthiest country in human history, with the means to easily provide healthcare to our entire population, tens of thousands of people die each year because they're priced out of the US health insurance market.[30]

Capitalism's death toll doesn't end there. The US killed several million people in the Korean War and Vietnam War in the name of "anti-communism."[31] The devastation wrought by the use of chemical weapons in Vietnam has led to widespread cancer and birth defects among the population, which persists to this day—that's when peasants aren't being blown up by land mines left behind by the US military.[32] The US also destroyed much of Cambodian society with its bombing campaign under the Nixon administration. This created a power vacuum into which Pol Pot and the murderous Khmer Rouge ascended.[33] And while the Khmer Rouge was slaughtering hundreds of thousands of peasants in Cambodia, the Indonesian military—backed by the US—was doing the same thing to the people of East Timor, wiping out one-third of the East Timorese population.[34] Right-wing regimes around the globe killed at least a few million more during the Cold War—with full US support. The US trained killers in Indonesia, Central America, and South America, and provided economic aid, weapons, intelligence, and diplomatic support to help carry out this mass murder program.[35]

Instead of pointing to atrocities committed by the worst regimes throughout history, and attempting to associate them with one's political opponents, we should instead be asking what these examples have in common. As Amartya Sen and Jean Drèze have written, in the case of the Chinese famine, blame should be attributed to the totalitarian political climate—in particular the lack of a free press—that characterized Mao's regime, not the fact that the Chinese economy was communist.[36] This should lead us to conclude that democratic accountability is necessary to force those in power to ensure vital resources reach the population. And it's why we should place such accountability at the forefront of our demands, and favor economic and political institutions that bring about a more democratic society. The right makes no such commitment, however. They attempt to scare people into rejecting moderate reforms that would improve the lives of millions, and instead force them to accept the right's cruel brand of capitalism that places power into the hands of a tiny, unaccountable, corporate elite.

Liberal Fascism

Some on the right claim that fascism is "of the left."[37] The Nazis, according to the right, "hated capitalism" and "did not believe in private property."[38] The right notes similarities between fascist regimes and "leftist" historical figures like Woodrow Wilson and Franklin Roosevelt, who—like fascists—made extensive use of propaganda and favored authoritarian government and state economic management.[39] The right also points out that "Nazi" literally stands for National Socialism.[40] Indeed, the right claims that Hitler was himself a socialist who endorsed the Nazis' "25 Points" manifesto, which included several left-wing economic reforms.[41] Furthermore, according to the right, "left-wing" is synonymous with big government, and there's no better example of big government than fascism. But there are problems with each of these claims.

While it's true that in the early stages of fascism, some fascists denounced certain aspects of capitalism, it was an alliance with capitalists that allowed fascists to gain support and root themselves in the political system. In 1921, Italian Prime Minister Giovani Giolotti included Mussolini's Fascists in his electoral coalition, along with liberals and nationalists, in order to roll back prior gains made by socialists.[42] Mussolini's Blackshirts also helped Italian landowners beat up their socialist enemies and destroy socialist newspapers, clubs, and organizations.[43] When it came to picking sides between fascism and the left, capitalists had no problem joining with fascists.

Look at the makeup of German political parties during Hitler's rise to power and it's obvious which side the fascists were on. Most of the left in Germany came from the industrial working class and belonged to the Social Democrats or the Communist Party. German fascists, however, came from other social groups—rural farmers, workers who were not part of the labor movement, war veterans, the middle class, and conservatives—and belonged to the *Nazi* Party.[44] Fascism's supporters had little interest in helping the left defeat capitalism in either Germany or Italy. Rural farmers in Germany supported the Nazis not because they held left-wing economic views, but because they shared a hatred Jews and Marxists, and supported Nazi efforts to expand access to farmland through annexation. War veterans in Italy hated the left because the left didn't fully support the war effort in World War I. Conservatives, along with fascists from the middle class, hardly supported left-wing economic policies such as tax hikes and unemployment compensation.[45]

The most telling evidence that shows which side the fascists were on, however, is what fascists did once in power. In Italy, fascists rejected "progressive and confiscatory taxation" as "fiscal demagoguery that discourages initiative,"[46] cut taxes, adopted the gold standard, and balanced the nation's budget.[47] Fascists in Germany banned strikes, dissolved independent labor unions, lowered wages, and boosted capitalists' profits through arms build-ups. Fascists also pioneered what we now call privatization—in other words handing over public goods to private corporations for profit. Mussolini privatized the post office, railroads, telephone companies, and state life insurance companies. Hitler privatized banks, shipyards, railway lines, shipping lines, and welfare organizations.[48] Fascists did not, as Republican Senator Rand Paul has claimed, "not believe in private property." When Nazis confiscated property, they did so only from their political opponents, foreigners, and Jews.[49] It should also be noted that socialists were among the first to be shipped off to concentration camps—before Jews.[50]

Some on the right try to get around these facts. Paul, for example, argues that because all capitalists didn't exercise absolute control over the means of production under Nazi rule—for example, when hiring and firing employees or setting prices—the Nazi economy was socialist.[51] This is nonsense. The fact that one facet of a nation's economy doesn't fit a strict definition of "capitalist" does not make its economy socialist. It's also worth pointing out here that, while it's true that some capitalists were forced to temporarily relinquish a degree of control over their firms, they continued to maintain ownership of these firms; and that many capitalists in Germany welcomed Nazi efforts to replace market forces with state management because they would have otherwise been ruined by the Great Depression.[52]

Causing even more confusion, the right points to similarities between fascists and Progressive figures, such as Woodrow Wilson and FDR, who the right conflates with the left. Jonah Goldberg, for example, claims that Progressivism (and by association the left) was Fascist because progressives harassed, beat, spied upon, and threw dissenters in jail during the Wilson administration.[53] Goldberg leaves out, however, that when Progressives were directing the state to beat people up and toss them in jail for their political views, they were attacking *the left*, and doing so from *the right*.[54] Goldberg is referring to the First Red Scare, but only briefly mentions that socialists were among the Wilson administration's targets. Goldberg also confuses fascism with authoritarianism, which has characterized all types of governments throughout history, both on the left and the right.[55] Lastly, Goldberg leaves out that American support for fascism came primarily from the right—especially businessmen, some of whom allegedly recruited support for a fascist coup against FDR because they perceived him as too far left[56]—and that "free market" intellectuals like Ludwig von Mises expressed admiration for fascists because, according to Mises, they had temporarily "saved European civilization."[57]

But wait a second. Doesn't "Nazi" stand for National *Socialism*, and isn't socialism left-wing? No. Nazi does stand for National Socialism, but this form of "socialism" wasn't left-wing. When fascists denounced aspects of capitalism, they didn't do so from the left. They did so because they thought capitalists were insufficiently nationalistic and that capitalism was too materialistic—not because they shared views with the left, such as the idea that capital exploited labor or that workers should own the means of production. When fascists branded themselves as "socialists," they were trying to attach themselves to a popular idea, not because they shared substantive views with socialists about how the economy should be organized.[58]

In order to distort the truth, the right cherry-picks evidence. Paul points to senior Nazi official Gregor Strasser, who held left-wing economic views.[59] But he leaves out that Strasser and other Nazis who held left-wing views were purged as the Nazis rooted themselves in the political system.[60]

If one wants to cherry-pick evidence, one can find any number of examples to show the opposite of what the right claims. Hitler claimed, for example, that, "Communism is not Socialism. Marxism is not Socialism. The Marxians have stolen the term and confused its meaning. I shall take Socialism away from the Socialists. Socialism, unlike Marxism, does not repudiate private property."[61] He also claimed that, "The main plank in the National Socialist program is to abolish the liberalistic concept of the individual and the Marxist concept of humanity and to substitute therefore the folk community, rooted in the soil and bound together by the bond of its common blood."[62]

As Hitler's words illustrate, National Socialists aimed to promote an extreme form of nationalism. The National Socialists' "socialism" emphasized solidarity based not on class, but on nationality, whereby those within the nation would be subordinated to the interests of the collective. This form of collectivism, however, wasn't left-wing. Fascist collectivism meant keeping the nation's existing economic order intact, based on the belief that doing so would benefit the nation.[63] If anything, this is a right-wing form of collectivism.

Finally, the right tries to associate fascism and the left by tying both to "big government." Because the left favors progressive taxation and a large welfare state, which is big government, and because fascist regimes are also a form of big government, fascism and the left are the same, according to the right. Big government is not the same as a government with a large welfare state, however. If a government cracks down on dissent, tortures and murders its citizens, shuts down the press, undermines free elections, and so on, but doesn't institute a large welfare state, would anyone deny this to be a form of big government? Of course not. The point of denigrating government as "big" is to draw attention to its oppressive nature, not the fact that it has a large state apparatus that provides public services. But it's understandable why the right would try to define big government in this way. The right has supported any number of regimes that have employed the type of state repression described above, including nearly every country in Latin America, and often did so with the help of former Nazis who escaped justice after World War II.[64]

The terms "left" and "right" don't refer to "big government" and "small government." Rather, "left" refers to an economic and political system under which we might expect a more egalitarian distribution of wealth, and "right" refers to one under which we might expect a more unequal, or hierarchical, distribution of wealth.[65] Fascists were therefore on the right. They aimed to restrict material wealth to their own nation and race, supported an unequal distribution of wealth within their nation, and repressed the left in order to maintain this distribution.

The right's attempt to associate the left with fascism rests on multiple layers of deception. The right redefines capitalism to fit with their "Nazis were anti-capitalist" narrative, lumps the left in with right-wing Progressives in order to associate the left with authoritarianism, equivocates when using the word "socialism" to associate the left with a form of right-wing nationalism, quote-mines fascist leaders to make it seem as if fascism was left-wing, and defines "big government" as being synonymous with the left in order to mask the right's support for authoritarian government. These are the types of mental gymnastics the right must go through when there are literal Neo-Nazis marching in the streets to support the right's political leaders. No amount of sophistry should distract us from the right's authoritarianism, its fascist tendencies, or the immorality of any system that's rooted in political or economic inequality.

Venezuela

According to the right, we shouldn't implement social-democratic welfare programs in the US because these programs are "socialism," and socialism doesn't work. The right claims that in order to see why, we need look no further than Venezuela. In the 1970s, Venezuela was one of the richest countries in Latin America. It was then taken over by a socialist "dictatorship," first under Hugo Chávez, now Nicholás Maduro, according to the right. The result? Food shortages, hyperinflation, political corruption, widespread social unrest, and state repression. A closer look at the factors that led to Venezuela's current economic situation, however, says more about the problems with capitalism.

The Venezuelan economy is capitalist, not socialist. In order to see why, we can look at a number of economic indicators, such as government spending as a percentage of GDP, the percentage of the population employed by the government, the percentage of Venezuela's economy that's publicly owned, the rate of unionization among Venezuela's workforce, and the percentage of co-ops in Venezuela's economy. Venezuela's numbers are relatively small compared to what we might expect in a socialist economy—in most cases smaller than countries like Denmark, Norway, Finland, or even France and Germany, none of which have seen their economies collapse.[66] Venezuela's private sector even grew relative to its public sector from 1999 to 2012.[67] What's funny is that when the Venezuelan economy boomed from 2003 to 2008 under Hugo Chávez, Fox News published an article pointing out that Venezuela was capitalist, wanting to give capitalism credit for Venezuela's economic success during this period (Venezuela's economy continued to boom until 2013).[68] While Venezuela's top elected officials may be self-described socialists, this doesn't make its economy socialist.

Nor do Venezuela's economic problems stem from its "socialist" policies. These problems stemmed from the failure of its political leadership to anticipate easily foreseeable economic obstacles. Venezuela's economic managers squandered the country's oil revenue by failing to bank reserves or invest in other economic sectors, which could have provided resources to smooth out the business cycle during economic downturns. Countries like Norway—which again, is more "socialist" than Venezuela—also rely on huge oil reserves, and have managed to avoid these problems.[69]

Venezuela's political leaders also failed to anticipate the power of the United States to strangle Venezuela's economy. In 2017, the US leveled sanctions that kept Venezuela from borrowing money in US financial markets, which prevented Venezuela from restructuring its foreign debt and made it impossible for the country to recover from the deep recession that began in 2013. Limits on borrowing also reduced Venezuela's oil production because Venezuela couldn't finance maintenance costs and new investment to ramp up production. This in turn led to losses in foreign exchange from oil exports, which was the primary culprit that contributed to Venezuela's hyperinflation. In 2019, further sanctions cut off Venezuela from US oil markets (35.6 percent of Venezuela's exports)—causing further losses in foreign exchange—and froze billions of dollars of Venezuelan assets held abroad that could have been used to stabilize its economy.[70] The US has also tried to foment a number of military coups, recognized a parallel government in the country, and has cast doubt on the legitimacy of Venezuelan presidential elections, creating political instability.

The right also ignores the progress made under Chávez and other Latin American countries that have adopted socialist policies. Before Chávez, poverty and illiteracy were far more widespread. Chávez reduced poverty by 49 percent and extreme poverty by 63 percent, reduced inequality, and expanded access to education, public pensions, housing, and healthcare. Contrast this with the two decades prior to Chávez, when income growth was negative.[71] If Venezuelan "socialism" is so bad, then this says more about capitalism, under which the poor in Venezuela fared worse. Similarly, Ecuador grew its economy by an average of 2.8 percent from 2007-2014, cut poverty by 30 percent, and expanded access to education and healthcare, while at the same time reducing its debt. Bolivia and Nicaragua have achieved similar outcomes, despite lacking the same resources as Venezuela.[72] All Venezuela's economic problems show is that the US has the power to crush weaker nations who attempt to show an alternative economic model to the right's brand of "free market" capitalism.

Technological Development

The right argues that all the great technology we have today—computers, iPhones, apps, and so on—are the result of capitalism. Under capitalism, entrepreneurs pair up with investors who risk their capital to develop these technologies. We're told that the level of technology we see today isn't possible in any other economic system. Those who criticize capitalism and want to redistribute wealth should either get off their iPhones or stop complaining. When the government taxes business, this leaves fewer funds for investment, hampers innovation, and leaves society worse off. We should instead keep taxes low and regulation to a minimum, allow capitalists to do their thing, and sit back and enjoy the benefits of innovation. The story of capitalist innovation, however, isn't as straightforward as the right claims.

Capitalism obviously leads to investment in new technology. Capitalist firms must re-invest part of their revenue to reduce the future costs of production, gain an advantage over their competitors, maintain steady profits, and repeat this process continually if they want to survive. This process has led to all sorts of labor-saving technology that has made life better for much of humanity. However, capitalism has hardly been sufficient to develop much of the advanced technology that exists today (more on this below). This is because the scale of investment required to develop advanced technology isn't possible without massive state funding. The cost to develop this technology is far greater than any single firm can bear, and because investors are risk averse and prefer short-term gains to long-term gains that may only materialize decades in the future—if at all—capitalists often need the state to bear the initial risk of investment and sustain the conditions needed for long-term research and development.

What are we talking about? How about interchangeable parts, transistors (which form the basis of modern electronics), the Internet, touch screens, the graphical user interface, voice recognition, lasers, satellite communication, biotechnology, mapping the Human Genome, computers, pharmaceutical drugs, nanotechnology, Google's search algorithm, jet engines, nuclear power, green technology, space travel to get satellites into Earth's orbit, lithium batteries, WiFi, LCD screens, GPS, cellular communications standards, computer programming languages, speech recognition technology, radar, the list goes on. These technologies were developed with tax dollars funneled through the military-industrial complex, or Xerox PARC and Bell Labs (both monopolies co-financed by the government). Capitalists only came in and commercialized these technologies after the government reduced the risk of investment, often long after private firms failed to see the value of these technologies.[73] A notable example involves AT&T and IBM, who missed their chance to privatize the Internet because they viewed it as unprofitable.[74]

The government also subsidizes innovation in other ways. During the early stages of economic development in the US, corporations relied on state credit to amass the enormous sums of capital needed to build a transport network and foster commerce. Private capital markets could not have underwritten the mammoth state canal systems created in the early nineteenth century, even if they had promised enough profit to attract private investors. Businesses have also relied on the US Postal Service, and later the national highway system, to transport goods to consumers over long distances. Millions of small businesses also receive loans from the government. Indeed, commerce would grind to a halt without a stable money supply—provided by a federally-chartered central bank—as well as counter-cyclical fiscal policy, which the government uses to boost demand during recessions. The government also insures bank deposits, which eliminates bank runs and keeps the financial system humming along. Not to mention intellectual property law, which "anarcho-capitalists" claim shouldn't be left to the government to enforce. And so on.

Capitalism is also often responsible for stifling innovation. Corporations are notorious for lowering prices temporarily in order to stamp out competition, or buying out their competition, often with the aim of shuttering new technology they don't see an advantage in adopting. The fossil fuel industry has long tried to destroy alternative energy—for example, electric cars, as well wind and solar power. Corporations also buy up patents en masse to prevent competitors from developing new technology with which they might have to compete. Corporations are also well known for developing products designed to break down after a period of time, so consumers will have to purchase these items again in the future—a strategy known as planned obsolescence, or in the case of software, programmed obsolescence. Ever wonder why your iPhone starts running slow after a new software update? That's why.[75] This should make it easy to see why cutting taxes and regulations isn't a great idea. These policies only further entrench the power of incumbent corporations, who would have even more resources at their disposal to implement anti-competitive business strategies and extract more wealth from society. The right doesn't want to foster innovation. They want capitalism to cannibalize itself while they sit back and funnel as much wealth into their pockets as they can.

Crony Capitalism

Capitalism has unleashed untold destruction on the world. It's created widespread poverty, exploited the most vulnerable members of society, destroyed the environment, led to countless military conflicts, corrupted our politics, shredded our social fabric, and undermined democracy. To absolve capitalism from its role in these evils, the right shifts blame elsewhere. They distinguish capitalism from "crony capitalism." According to the right, economic inequality, political corruption, and other social ills many attribute to capitalism aren't really due to capitalism. Rather, these issues are caused by the government's perversion of capitalism, which happens when the government expands its regulatory apparatus, which is easily captured by big business. It's therefore unfair to criticize capitalism and unwise to implement social programs to solve the "problems" of capitalism. Instead, we should make the government "smaller" by cutting these programs, reducing taxes, slashing regulations, and solving society's problems through competition in the free market. The right's take, however, is a laughably naive.

When the right cites examples of "crony capitalism," they mean obvious examples of corruption—lobbying and campaign expenditures in return for favorable regulation (or lack of regulation), subsidies, and so on. In order to prevent this from happening, the right claims we need to make the government "small." Less government, less corruption, we're told. But capitalism's problems have little to do with these obvious examples of corruption compared to the core functions of the state the right favors. Are property rights crony capitalism? Is the enforcement of contracts crony capitalism? Are corporate charters crony capitalism? Most of the right would answer no. Yet without "big government"—taxation, redistribution, and regulation—the core functions of a capitalist state make political corruption inevitable. Once we establish a "small" government, and use this form of government to create the legal basis for capitalist firms to exist, firms that gain an initial advantage can easily undercut or buy out their competitors and consolidate their market share. These firms quickly accumulate wealth, which they can use to corrupt the government. Indeed, the smaller the government relative to the size of industry, the *easier* it is to corrupt.

This isn't all. For capitalism to develop on any significant scale, it needs an *activist* state—to invest in infrastructure, protect infant industries from foreign competition, subsidize technological innovation, create a stable money supply, boost consumer demand, and so on. This is the only way capitalist economies have ever developed. What the right won't admit is that an economic system that requires such a powerful state in order not only to exist, but to develop on any significant scale, leaves itself open to cronyism. Without counter-balancing institutions that redistribute wealth and regulate industry, capitalism becomes controlled by the very thing it creates. In other words, "small government" inevitably leads to big government. Once this process is set in motion, there's no mechanism powerful enough to stop it other than the government itself. *This* is why the right aims to keep the government "small." The government is (in theory) accountable to workers and communities, and the right doesn't want the population to interfere with the prerogatives of private enterprise. The right's "solution" to crony capitalism is therefore limited to tax cuts and deregulation, which only makes the problem worse. When the government cuts taxes and regulations, it doesn't care about the prevailing distribution of property and power. If this distribution is highly skewed, the state perpetuates economic inequality via its enforcement of property rights, and leaves those with the most wealth and power with even more resources.

But can we expand government without having to accept high levels of corruption? This question is easy to answer. Other nations have implemented more expansive social welfare states and have managed to regulate industry to a larger degree than the US, yet they have lower levels of political corruption. There's no reason we can't follow their example. The key is to create institutions that greatly reduce economic inequality, make an ongoing effort to hold the government accountable to the public, and limit the possibility of economic inequality from arising. Capitalism does the opposite. There's no difference between capitalism and "crony capitalism."

CHAPTER FIVE

Economics 101

The right claims that liberals and the left don't understand how the economy works. If they did, they wouldn't claim that poverty or income stagnation are a problem in the US, or claim that the government can solve these so-called problems by taxing the productive members of society and using this wealth to create social welfare programs. These flawed policies supposedly destroy wealth and ultimately reduce living standards in the long run. Only the free market can raise living standards, we're told, which liberals and the left would know if they just understood "Economics 101."

Just look at the so-called poor in America. The right points out that the "poor" walk around with cell phones, have cable TV, and eat lobster for dinner. Even the kings of yesteryear didn't have these luxuries, so there's little reason to be concerned, and no reason to implement social welfare programs aimed at alleviating poverty, or to raise taxes in order to pay for these programs. Indeed, according to the right, the reason the poor have it so good is because capitalism fosters innovation that improves living standards. Taxing wealth short-circuits this process, and thereby leaves us worse off.

But even if poverty were a problem, according to the right, this isn't due to the poor receiving insufficient income or being denied access to resources like education and healthcare; it's due to a lack of "personal responsibility" on the part of the poor. There's plenty of opportunity in the US. Just look at Oprah! She grew up poor, yet has become one of the most successful people in America. There's no reason others can't be like her. If the poor don't take advantage of the opportunities life provides them, it's their problem, not society's.

The right raises similar objections to concerns over income stagnation. They point to the fact that the upper-middle class has expanded in recent decades, which—again—shows it's possible for anyone to move up the income ladder. Not only this, but statistics that measure income stagnation also fail to take rising living standards into account, as well as the fact that families are smaller than they used to be, which means they need less income. Once again, it's unfair that 60 percent of the population "gets more back" than they pay in taxes while others have to foot the bill.

But even if we wanted to alleviate problems like poverty and income stagnation, this is impossible in the long run, according to the right. The US has already spent $30 trillion on social welfare programs, yet we still have poverty. This supposedly shows that we're just wasting money on these programs, which in any case are unsustainable. If we keep increasing spending on social welfare programs at the current rate, pretty soon we'll simply run out of "other peoples' money." Those who don't understand this just lack "common sense."

But what about countries like Sweden and Denmark? Haven't these countries been able to successfully implement generous social welfare programs, and doesn't this show it's possible for the US to do the same? Not according to the right, which claims that the only reason the Nordic countries are able to maintain larger welfare states is because they're either small, or they're "culturally homogeneous," both of which supposedly make it easier to build a popular consensus in favor of social programs; and because these countries rely on the US to maintain security around the world, which allows other countries to spend less on their militaries and more on social programs. The US doesn't have this luxury.

The right is wrong on each of these points. Not being poor, for example, has nothing to do with having cell phones and being able to eat out at Red Lobster every once in a while. To meet basic needs in our society, individuals have to pay for rent, food, clothing, healthcare, child care, etc. on a monthly basis, and they must earn enough income to do so. But much of the population simply can't earn income. If you're a child, a student, disabled, or too old, you can't (or shouldn't have to) work. For millions of others, the US economy doesn't create enough well-paying jobs to provide them with sufficient income. This has devastating effects on families—especially children, whose human potential is limited without access to economic security, a good education, a safe home, an environment free of crime and violence, healthcare, and so on.

Similarly, the right's excuses for income stagnation distract from the fact that, absent policies favored by the right, the poor and middle class would be taking home more income and wealth, and society would have more than it needs to provide resources like healthcare and education to all who need it. Indeed, the "free stuff" the poor currently receive from government transfers pales in comparison to the stuff elites receive—not only from tax breaks, but from the market economy, which is rigged heavily in their favor. It follows that when higher earners are made to pay a slightly higher tax rate, this isn't an unfair burden society forces on them. The rich get to keep most of the stuff markets distribute to them, while the public only recovers a small portion of this stuff through higher taxes on the rich—which aren't that high.

Nor is it true that social welfare programs are somehow uniquely difficult to implement in the US. A number of these programs—like Social Security—already exist in the US, and are not only effective at reducing poverty, but remain widely popular. Countries with larger welfare states don't have them because they're "culturally homogeneous" or because they're smaller. As we'll see, smaller countries face many impediments that larger countries like the US don't. Yet these countries were able to implement large welfare states without the harmful consequences the right warns us about.

The reason poverty still persists in the US is because the right has done everything they can to attack the welfare state and concentrate economic power in the hands of a tiny elite. The right then cynically claims we should abandon efforts to expand the welfare state because it "doesn't work." Social ills such as poverty and economic inequality, however, are policy choices, not the result of some sort of iron law we can't overcome.

Poverty

The right claims that poverty isn't really a problem in the US. Compared to past societies, the poor have it good. They have cell phones, air conditioning, microwaves, TVs, and eat lobster dinners. What do they have to complain about? In any case, poverty isn't *society's* problem. If someone is poor, it's because they supposedly lack "personal responsibility." If people would just graduate high school, get a job, and wait to get married before having kids, they wouldn't be poor. If we want to solve the "problem" of poverty, why not encourage individuals to do these things rather than give them government handouts? The right also points to the success of West Indian blacks, as well as Asian and Jewish Americans, to show that poverty comes from culture and individual choices, not broader societal factors. The right, however, couldn't be more wrong about poverty.

Poverty is indeed a problem in the US. Those who experience poverty are likely to be less healthy, live shorter lives, and must endure constant stress, as well as the burden of harmful social stigmas. They're more likely to be victims of violence, crime, and predatory lending, and have far less access to quality housing and education.[1] The working poor are also forced to accept the worst jobs in society. They must often toil in dangerous factories, processing plants, or agricultural labor camps performing backbreaking labor, or must work in low-paid service industries. These workers are also more likely to suffer indignities on the job, such as harassment from their bosses, and are just one job loss, injury, or illness away from total ruin.[2] Poverty also has a particularly devastating effect on children. When they enter kindergarten, children from poor homes tend to have significantly lower cognitive and non-cognitive skills than children from affluent homes. They perform worse in school, are far more likely to end up poor as adults, are more likely to grow up surrounded by violence, drugs, and crime, and more likely to suffer emotional or physical trauma. These factors severely limit their human potential.[3]

Even if only a small fraction of the US population were poor, we should do everything we can to eradicate poverty, given the problems outlined above. But in the US, millions of people suffer from poverty.

Nearly 18 percent of the population lives below the poverty line at any given time and nearly twenty percent of children are poor.[4] About 10 percent of children spend at least half their childhood living in poverty.[5] This is a national disgrace.

But compared to past societies, don't the "poor" still have it good? The right points out that the poor don't have to worry about the high levels of infant mortality or disease, nor do they have to endure the type of drudgery, or the dearth of food that feudal peasants once endured. Indeed, in many ways they live better than kings once did.

To see why this claim is so ridiculous, try to imagine if you and your spouse brought home a combined $20,335 while trying to raise a child. This was the official poverty threshold in 2019 for a family of three. Now imagine if you and your spouse only brought home $10,178 or less. That's what 45 percent of poor families took home in income in 2019. Contrast these numbers with what most people think they need to meet their basic needs. When asked what the smallest amount of money a family of four needs to bring in each year to get by, the average amount given by those polled is $58,000.[6] Yet the poverty threshold for a family of four is less than half that amount. These statistics suggest poverty is a much bigger problem than the right imagines.

But even if the standard by which we determine how to distribute resources in society should be based on how well the recipients of these resources live relative to someone who lived two- or three-hundred years ago, then let's follow this argument to its logical conclusion. If the poor are living like kings, then the rich are living like gods. If we raised taxes on the rich, they would still have higher living standards than Louis XIV, as well as the "kings" who live in poverty today. The right's argument therefore supports soaking the rich. Unless the right wants to do that, they should refrain from using fallacious arguments to justify denying resources to the poor.

What about the idea that high rates of poverty in the US are due to a "culture of poverty" among the poor, like single mothers having children out of wedlock to collect welfare benefits instead of getting a job? This claim is also ridiculous. The poor in America aren't just single mothers who don't work. About two-thirds of the poor aren't even eligible to work because they're either retired, in school, disabled, or too young. Among the poor who *are* eligible to work, 63 percent are employed in paid labor. Some of these workers are employed in part-time labor, but many of them are caring for loved ones, can't find full-time work (employers increasingly avoid offering full-time work to avoid paying benefits to their employees), or have multiple part-time jobs.[7] Whether you're poor in America has little to do with having children out of wedlock or not getting a job, unless we think toddlers should be employed sweeping floors at the local car dealership, or that individuals should have to work 3, 4, or 5 jobs to support a family.

Even if single mothers on welfare contributed significantly to America's poverty problem, there is plenty of evidence that shows we could eliminate poverty in ways that don't shame these people (who supposedly live large on $35 welfare checks they get for each kid, on average)[8] into getting jobs. In the US, the rate of single parenthood is around the OECD average, yet the poverty rate among single mothers in the US is much higher than it is in other OECD countries. Some of these countries, such as Iceland, Sweden, and Denmark, have even higher rates of single parenthood, but far lower poverty rates.[9] What these examples show is that, if we want to reduce poverty, there are other ways to accomplish this goal, for example by providing the type of robust social safety net found in these countries (more on this below).

But there's another problem with the right's "welfare queen" narrative. Blaming single mothers for poverty ignores obvious factors that explain why some people are poor in the US and others aren't.

Indeed, if it were true that single-parenthood is a primary driver of poverty in the US, how can it explain the fact that the median white single parent in the US has 2.2 times more wealth than the median black *two-parent* household?[10] Obviously there are far more significant factors at play when it comes to who is poor in America. Blacks, for example, were enslaved for hundreds of years, subject to Jim Crow for another hundred years, and remain disadvantaged by decades of housing discrimination, underfunded schools, and a lack of good jobs in their communities. This should be common sense.

Okay, but can't individuals lift themselves out of poverty by attaining a higher level of education? Wouldn't this translate to them getting better-paying jobs, and therefore more income, which they could use to provide for their families? Not so fast. The share of high school graduates has risen 26 percentage points among the bottom half of the income distribution over the past four decades, and 31 percent among the bottom quarter of the income distribution, while the share of four-year college graduates rose 10 percent and 7 percent in the same categories, respectively. Yet income has stagnated for these cohorts.[11] This is because we structure labor markets in the US to create low-paying (increasingly part-time) jobs that lack benefits. Around 40 percent of all US jobs in 2018 were low-paying jobs that paid less than $16 an hour. Nearly twice the proportion of full-time American workers have low-wage jobs compared to workers in other wealthy countries.[12] America's corporate aristocracy has used every trick in the book to boost the power of employers and undermine the power of workers, and they've been doing so for decades. They've supported tight monetary policy to generate unemployment, allowed the minimum wage to erode, entered into trade agreements that allow employers to offshore what were once highly-paid manufacturing jobs, and—perhaps most importantly—created or enforced laws in ways that allow employers to bust unions, which has fueled a precipitous decline in union membership and, as a result, eroded the power of workers to bargain for higher wages and benefits.[13]

It's worth noting why other countries have more well-paying jobs than we do in the US. These countries structure their labor markets in a much different way. They have laws that set a higher minimum wage. They provide every citizen with a debt-free college education. They provide workers generous unemployment benefits. They have stronger unions. They have sectoral bargaining and co-determination. And so on. All of these policies allow the working class as a whole to get ahead and bargain for higher wages and benefits. But the right supports none of these policies. It makes no sense to claim that poverty isn't a problem (since individuals can just attain a higher level of education if they wanted) while supporting a host of policies that undermine the power of the working class, unless you mean to trick the public into accepting an economic system that doesn't benefit them.

But here's the thing: even if workers got better jobs and the right weren't doing everything they could to undermine the power of workers, this wouldn't necessarily reduce poverty to the degree we want. What about children? The disabled? The elderly? Again, these people don't work. Higher pay for workers would mitigate this problem to some degree (higher pay might allow a worker, for example, to provide more resources to their dependents), but if we want to eliminate poverty, we need additional policies that distribute income to *everyone* who can't (or shouldn't) work. Luckily, other countries have figured out how to do this as well. They have universal public healthcare. They have guaranteed parental leave. They provide free child care. They provide more generous housing subsidies. They provide a child allowance. And so on. The same is true to some extent in the US, which all but eliminated poverty among the elderly by implementing Social Security.

These policies are the most effective means at our disposal to reduce poverty. We just choose not to go further.

But wait, don't these programs erode individual initiative, causing more people to earn less and become dependent on the government? Far from it. Income mobility is much higher in countries with more generous welfare states.[14] This only makes sense. If I (and my family) have more resources, I may not have to accept whatever crummy job that comes along just to be able to keep a roof over my family's head. Nor would I become trapped in a bad job, since I wouldn't risk losing benefits that are traditionally tied to employment, such as health insurance. With the resources provided by a strong welfare state, I would have more options available to me, which might include pursuing more education, training, or a better career; or perhaps starting my own business, since the financial risk associated with starting a business would be reduced. Some people may of course choose not to do these things. But on balance, insofar as income mobility serves as a proxy for individual initiative, the evidence suggests that a stronger welfare state *promotes* individual initiative.

But what about Asian Americans, Jewish Americans, and West Indian blacks? Haven't they had success relative to native-born blacks and Latinos—and even whites? And doesn't this prove you can make it in America if you just have the right cultural traits? Not at all. The right leaves out that a disproportionate number of those who count themselves among these groups are self-selected. Many of them were able to emigrate because they had more resources than others who live in their places of origin, or because they made extraordinary efforts to get here. Immigration quotas also ensure that only a small fraction of immigrants from more-populous countries are able to emigrate to the US, and because those who are allowed to emigrate are often selected based on their professional qualifications (and are therefore more likely to achieve economic success on average), this skews the educational attainment and income of these groups relative to other groups—Asians being the prime example.[15]

Look, no one denies there are individuals who can overcome economic hardship under the right circumstances, regardless of what "culture" they supposedly represent. The point, however, is that our economic system is structured in a way that guarantees only a small number of those who face economic hardship—those who happen to possess some arbitrary combination of traits that are beneficial in our current economic system—are likely to achieve economic success. And not all of these traits are good. Many immigrants who achieve success run small businesses and prosper by treating those who work for them (often their children, or others in their family networks who immigrate) little better than slaves. They pay them extremely low wages, or in the case of their children, often pay them nothing. We shouldn't strive to promote cultural traits that produce one-dimensional, petty tyrants whose primary concern is to scrounge as much wealth as they can while exploiting their own family because they faced deprivation prior to immigrating to the US. A culture that promotes these traits is psychotic. And what for? So those who accumulated wealth the easy way—by being born in the US, and likely into affluence—can maintain their wealth and privilege? Please.

Nor does anyone deny that you can find individuals among the poor who would make bad life choices (and adversely impact the lives of their children and families) no matter how many opportunities society provides them. But to show these individuals no compassion, or to deny others who face economic hardship—including the children of those who make bad life choices—the resources they need to live dignified lives, and ignore the structural impediments elites have created to prevent millions from living up to their human potential, is immoral.

The persistence of poverty isn't due to a culture of poverty among the poor, but a culture of entitlement among the affluent. This culture promotes selfishness, greed, indifference to the suffering of others, a lack of collective responsibility to right the wrongs of the past, a willful blindness to how our economy is structured, and an unwillingness to ensure that everyone in society enjoys access to resources that enable them to lead free and independent lives. The right can make up all the excuses they want, but poverty remains a major problem in the US. The right aims to make it seem otherwise in order to trick the rest of society into letting corporations and the rich hoard as much of society's wealth as possible, no matter how much poverty this creates, how much it harms individuals, or how much it limits our ability to fix society's problems.

Income Stagnation

The right claims that concerns over income stagnation are overblown. They point out that it's possible for some people to move from the bottom of America's income distribution to the top—just look at Oprah! Why can't others be more like her? But even if not everyone can have as much success as Oprah, not to worry. While individuals may start out earning very little income, they'll make more money as they advance in their careers. There's no need to redistribute income; everyone just has to pay their dues. The right also says those who are concerned over stagnating income don't count income such as employer benefits. If we include this form of income, the picture looks less dire. Furthermore, households have gotten smaller, so they don't *need* as much income. And finally, the right argues that concerns over stagnating income don't take into account the decrease in the cost of consumer goods, which supposedly offsets the cost of stagnating income. So is income stagnation even a problem?

Not if you like it when rich people steal your money. From the end of World War II until the early 1970s, incomes rose across the entire income distribution in the US. When productivity increased, so did wages. This is because workers had the power to demand higher wages and benefits. Since then, however, income has stagnated for the middle and lower class, while the top income decile has seen its income rise dramatically, with most of these gains concentrated among the top .01 percent of earners.[16] This is because elites have rigged our economic system to funnel more of society's income and wealth to themselves. Tight monetary policy, lax enforcement of labor laws, offshoring, industrial automation, letting the minimum wage erode, and so on, all diminish the bargaining power of the middle and lower class, preventing them from demanding higher pay.[17]

The right doesn't want you to understand this. Instead, they make up all sorts of excuses to trick people into letting the rich keep their outsized share of society's income and wealth. Take the claim that income mobility makes up for income inequality. We're told that if you want to earn more income, get a better job! Intergenerational income mobility in the US, however, is among the lowest in the developed world. While there might be some churn among top earners and those just below, relatively few people move from the bottom to the top, or vice versa, like we should expect if our society were truly meritocratic.[18] The fact that it's possible for a lucky few to move from the bottom to the top doesn't justify structuring our economy in a way that perpetuates this rigid class structure.

Even if it were true that income mobility was higher in the US, this wouldn't mean we shouldn't tax the rich to pay for social programs. Indeed, the possibility of income mobility provides a rationale to soak the rich. After all, if the rich were taxed more heavily, why can't they climb even higher up the income ladder in order to make up the difference?

What about *intra*-generational income mobility? Don't people move up the income ladder over the span of their career, and doesn't this mean we shouldn't be worried about economic inequality? No. While most people do move up the income distribution during their lifetime, the fact remains that *at any given point in your life* you're making less than you otherwise would if elites hadn't structured our economy to distribute income to those at the top.[19] Intragenerational income mobility doesn't justify letting the rich steal your money.

What about employer benefits such as health insurance and retirement contributions? According to the right, income has risen much faster than the naysayers claim, because we don't take this form of income into account. This claim is misleading, however. Those in the middle quintile of America's income distribution have seen very little increase in income even when including employer benefits. These benefits are concentrated among those in the top two quintiles.[20] This picture looks even bleaker when we consider what employer benefits get us. Increased income from employer sponsored health insurance pays for rising healthcare costs, not increased benefits. This income doesn't benefit workers; it just flows to hospital administrators, pharmaceutical executives, shareholders, insurers, doctors, and medical device manufacturers that comprise America's bloated health care system.

But shouldn't we care more about *household* income? Hasn't household income increased over the past several decades? No. Single-parent household income hasn't risen at all since the 1970s, and household income for two-parent households has risen only by adding a second earner as women entered the workforce in greater numbers.[21] To make matters worse, it's mostly women who have to both work and manage household production (doing laundry, cooking dinner, etc.). The fact that more women work also means households have new expenses like daycare. Household income also flattened out once female workforce participation reached its peak in the year 2000.[22]

But haven't households gotten smaller over the past several decades? And doesn't this mean they need less income? No. Households have gotten smaller for the rich as well, but their incomes have increased at the expense of households at the bottom.[23]

What about TVs? Focusing on income doesn't take lower prices for consumer goods into account, which leave consumers with more money in their pockets. Shouldn't this make us less concerned about income stagnation? No. There's no evidence that we have to sacrifice slower income growth in order to receive the benefits of new technology. In the 1940s, 50s, and 60s, those at the bottom of the income distribution saw their incomes grow at roughly the same pace as the economy, while still benefiting from new technology.[24] Even more problematic is the fact that while Americans are paying less for TVs today, they're paying more for automobiles, housing, healthcare, and education. These costs have risen faster than inflation, eating up a larger share of household income. Not only this, but because families have shifted from one earner to two earners, they often have to add childcare, as well as a second automobile, to their expenses. In order to be able to afford these costs, households have taken on more debt, which rose from 74 percent of their disposable income in 1970 to 138 percent in 2007.[25] Lower prices for consumer goods only offset these costs to a degree.

The litany of excuses the right offers to justify economic inequality is downright comical. No matter how the right wants to spin it, we're all getting screwed. The right makes these excuses to prevent the rest of us from sharing in the wealth we all help create. Instead, the right wants the rich to be able to hog this wealth for themselves.

Free Stuff

The right claims that social welfare programs constitute "free stuff" doled out by the government. The bottom 60 percent of the population "gets more back" than they pay in taxes, according to the right, which is supposedly unfair. Leftist politicians use "handouts" to "buy" votes from those who refuse to provide for themselves. Conversely, those who don't receive this free stuff *earn* what they get in the market. When Republicans cut taxes for the rich, they're not giving stuff away, but letting hardworking individuals keep more of their own money, according to the right. But in reality, the "free stuff" distributed to the poor are crumbs compared to the free stuff the affluent receive.

The entire history of the US is one example after another of its most privileged members stealing from those with lesser means, and using the government to help them do it. White settlers used the government to help wipe out America's indigenous peoples, allowing whites to squat on Native American land. White men then used the government to selectively enforce individual rights, allowing whites to exploit blacks, women, Native Americans, and immigrants. Without this selective enforcement of rights, lazy plantation owners, mine operators, railroad barons, and factory bosses would have had to pick their own tobacco and cotton fields, spin the cotton into cloth, mine their own coal, lay railroad tracks, or man dangerous machinery.

The same is true today. Our economic system is rigged to concentrate wealth into the hands of corporations and the rich, gifting them the private power to steal from those with lesser means, as well as from society. In prior chapters, we saw how elites have structured our institutions over centuries to funnel the wealth society produces into the hands of elites. We've also seen that most of the wealth society generates today is derived from the efforts of those who came before us, along with the institutions we've inherited. This wealth should belong to all of us, yet we hand it over to a small sliver of society. Every penny of this wealth is free stuff that those who make up this sliver of society didn't earn.

We've also seen how the government continues to diminish the power of workers on behalf of capital by failing to enforce legal protections for workers, keeping interest rates high to "fight inflation" (and therefore generate unemployment), allowing the minimum wage to erode, signing trade agreements to allow corporations access to cheap labor elsewhere, enacting so-called right-to-work laws that drain union funding, slashing spending on social programs, and so on.[26]

Indeed, we've seen that the very structure of American government is a massive subsidy to the affluent. The "checks and balances" built into our government provide the rich with a number of advantages that allow them to thwart political reforms favored by those with little economic power. Equal state representation in the Senate gives more power to less-populous, Republican-leaning states, which are more friendly to business interests. The Senate filibuster adds another barrier to popular reform by raising the threshold of votes needed for the majority party to pass legislation. The President possesses additional veto power over Congress. The Electoral College handicaps Democratic voters when selecting the President. Partisan gerrymandering handicaps Democratic voters when selecting members of the House. These advantages can only be overcome by large majorities, which have become nearly impossible given the influence of money in American politics. Even if we were to overcome these barriers and pass reforms meant to alter the balance of power in society, the courts can veto these reforms to keep the gravy train of free stuff flowing to the rich.[27]

The affluent also receive free stuff in a number of other ways. Corporate welfare, primarily funneled through the military-industrial complex, benefits large defense contractors, their investors, as well as top-level managers and engineers.[28] Immigration policy creates a class of exploitable non-citizens within the US, allowing employers to pay them peanuts compared to what they would pay citizens.[29] Tax expenditures subsidize mortgage payments, health insurance plans, and retirement accounts of the affluent. The government taxes income from owning financial assets, as well as inherited wealth, at lower rates than other forms of income.[30] Immigration quotas, medical school and law school admissions, and licensing requirements restrict the supply of doctors and lawyers, boosting their salaries.[31] The amount of free stuff the beneficiaries of these policies receive is endless.

While underprivileged populations in theory have access to this free stuff, in practice they're in no position to benefit. The conservative nanny state instead helps the affluent, who are better positioned to capitalize on opportunities that lead to lucrative careers, and access to better social networks and other perks, so they accumulate stuff far more easily than others. In order to maintain this system, all the rich have to do is break out their checkbooks every once in a while, or rely on the wealthiest members of America's corporate aristocracy, to bankroll politicians who will protect the interests of the rich. Meanwhile, the rest of the population is left with crumbs. The right doesn't care about free stuff. They only object when other people get free stuff, because they want to hog all of society's stuff for themselves.

Moochers

The right claims that the rich bear a greater tax burden than the rest of society. Indeed, almost half of the country are "moochers" who live off the sacrifice of the rich. To support this claim, the right points out that

47 percent of those who file taxes pay no federal income tax, and that the bottom 60 percent of the population "gets more back" than they pay in taxes. According to the right, this is supposed to show that higher taxes on the rich are unfair. We should therefore cut taxes on the rich. About two seconds of reflection, however, shows why this claim is nonsense.

Let's first note that the claim that "47 percent of Americans pay no federal income tax" is misleading. The right leaves out that everyone pays state, payroll, and consumption taxes. Indeed, these taxes eat up a larger share of income for the poor than they do for the rich. Focusing on federal income taxes also ignores that the rich receive income from the shares of companies they own, capital gains, retirement accounts, inheritance, and so on, which are taxed at lower rates than income from employment. When accounting for all such taxes, the US tax system is only slightly progressive, and for the highest earners is actually *regressive*. The poor pay about 28 percent of their income in taxes, the middle class pays 25 percent, the upper middle class pays 30 percent, the top .01 percent pays 34 percent, and the top 400 families pay only 23 percent.[32] The right therefore paints a grossly distorted picture of who actually pays taxes and how much they pay.

Now, why does it make little sense to complain that the rich pay "so much more" in taxes? If someone makes $500,000 annually and pays $200,000 in taxes, and another person makes $20,000 annually but pays $1,000 in taxes, which of these individuals bears a greater tax burden? It's the person who's taxed $1,000. After taxation the person making $500,000 still has $300,000 whereas the person making $20,000 is only left with $19,000. This is because the rich receive so much more income *before* taxes and everyone else receives so little. Well, "Duh!" you might think. Doesn't the person making $500,000 *deserve* their income? Not at all. The US economy is structured in a way that distributes the bulk of society's wealth to a small minority of the population, and does so in an arbitrary fashion. Our laws are set up to distribute resources through markets, while at the same time concentrating market power in the hands of large corporations and their shareholders. This allows corporations and the rich to appropriate wealth on the backs of workers—and society.

What are some of the ways they do this? The government makes it easier for companies to bust unions, administers monetary policy to generate unemployment, enters into trade agreements that allow corporations to offshore jobs, allows the minimum wage to erode, and provides only a threadbare social safety net to protect workers, making them more dependent on their employers. When individual workers attempt to bargain with their employers for higher pay and benefits under these conditions, the employers have the advantage, and can therefore pay workers less. These lower wages and salaries function like a private tax on income employees would otherwise receive if the system weren't rigged against them.[33] Yet the right has tricked large swaths of the population into believing that tax rates are a barometer by which to measure the fairness of our economic system.

There's no reason the economy should be set up to funnel so much of society's wealth to a small sliver of the population. It doesn't benefit society. It just dilutes the agency of ordinary citizens, and encourages those with more power to corrupt the government and further enrich themselves at everyone else's expense. Who gets more back from the government in this scenario? The rich, of course. It's the government—legislatures, courts, police, etc.—that make and enforce laws that distribute resources overwhelmingly to the rich. Not only do the rich bear less of a tax burden—because they make so much money—but *everyone else is paying taxes for a system that overwhelmingly benefits the rich*. It's the rich who are the moochers.

The Welfare State

The right claims that social-democratic welfare programs are doomed to fail in the US. They point out that we've spent $30 trillion to fight poverty, yet we still have poverty. They claim that social spending is growing to unsustainable levels, which will lead to less innovation, and make society poorer in the long run. They claim the only reason other countries can institute large welfare states is because they're smaller, or because they're "culturally homogeneous," which allows them to more easily build a consensus in favor of social programs. The right also claims that these countries have more to spend on social programs because they rely on the US to protect them, and therefore have smaller military budgets. Even if we tried to tax the rich to pay for similar programs in the US, the right claims, the rich would just find a way to avoid paying these taxes. Therefore, we might as well just give up on trying to institute a large welfare state and instead rely on economic growth and private charity to meet society's needs. All of these claims, however, are belied by the evidence.

Social-democratic welfare programs have not only enjoyed widespread success all over the world, but also in the US. Social Security reduces poverty among the elderly from around 40 percent to less than 10 percent.[34] Tax credits and transfers continue to cut the overall poverty rate by 35 percent every year.[35] Other countries that have a more robust social welfare state have all but eliminated poverty.[36] These programs not only reduce current levels of poverty but also do so well into the future. Universal basic income programs in Canada, Native American reservations in the United States, and villages in Africa show that those who received these benefits were more likely to graduate, get a good job, and enjoy higher long-term earnings, which enables them to "pay back" the government when the higher income they receive as a result is eventually taxed. We have known the same thing about funding public education for years.[37]

Why, then, do we still have poverty? Because capitalism as it currently exists in the US *generates poverty on an ongoing basis*. Elites are constantly rigging our economy to distribute wealth to themselves, undercutting our ability to end poverty. The Federal Reserve has instituted tight monetary policy since the early 1980s, creating unemployment under the guise of "fighting inflation" or creating "flexible" labor markets. Anti-labor policies have all but destroyed unions. Corporations have offshored jobs, or introduced automation to replace workers. The government has cut public assistance for single mothers. We've allowed the minimum wage to erode dramatically. And so on. These policies—and others—leave millions without sufficient income and make workers dependent on employers who don't pay them enough to escape poverty.[38]

In order to get around this problem, the right tries to make it seem as if a large social-democratic welfare state isn't feasible in the long run. Nicholas Eberstadt of the right-wing American Enterprise Institute wrote a book claiming that the outlay for entitlements in 2012 was 100 times more than it was in 1960, growing at an average rate of 9.5 percent each year. According to Eberstadt, this was evidence of a growing "nation of takers" that can't possibly be sustained.[39] If this were true, we should indeed be worried. But as economist Brad DeLong has shown, Eberstadt's analysis is wildly misleading.

Eberstadt uses irrelevant statistics to paint a distorted picture of America's welfare state. For one, he compares spending levels in 1960 to 2012 spending levels in absolute terms, rather than as a percentage of the economy. This is misleading because it doesn't reflect economic growth. Because the economy has grown steadily over the past six decades, we have more money to spend on social programs than we did in 1960. Nor does Eberstadt account for population growth. We have more people today than in the 1960s. This means we would spend more money today even if we spent the same amount (or even less) per person. As DeLong points out, increased spending isn't evidence of a growing nation of takers, but simply of a growing nation. Nor does Eberstadt account for inflation. The cost of Eberstadt's welfare state has only grown in nominal terms, not real terms. Nor does Eberstadt account for rising health care costs. This is important to point out because while it's true that spending on healthcare has grown, this isn't because people are "taking" more, but because America's bloated healthcare system takes more. When accounting for these factors, DeLong found that spending growth came to 1.2 percent per year, not 9.5—hardly evidence of a growing nation of takers.[40]

But what about healthcare? Isn't increased public spending on healthcare still a problem? For the sake of argument, let's say it is. What's the solution? We know other countries that have public health insurance systems spend around half as much per person as America's mostly private health insurance system. It's easy to see why. Private health insurers have high administrative costs, waste money on advertising, must make a profit, and don't have the same bargaining power as the government to bid down prices for hospital care, pharmaceuticals, and advanced medical devices. If we want to spend less on healthcare, the solution is *more* government, not less. Indeed, we already spend more on healthcare than we would with a single-payer health insurance system. If we spent this money instead on a single-payer system, we could pay for everyone's health care and still have billions left over.[41]

But what about other programs? Won't more spending on existing programs—along with new programs like free college, universal pre-K, a child allowance, etc.—lead to less innovation, as more money is diverted away from investment in new technology? Don't the countries with larger welfare states show this to be true? Aren't these countries free-riding on innovation from America, which has lower social spending and a more favorable business climate? Hardly. When the right tries to show that the US is more innovative, they often cite statistics showing the US issues more patents than other countries. But what does this actually show? Most US patents are bought by large companies in order to stifle competition, which *reduces* innovation.[42] This is the inevitable outcome of the right's preferred brand of capitalism. Cutting taxes and regulations helps concentrate economic power into the hands of fewer and fewer corporations, enabling them to employ a host of anti-competitive business tactics.

Moreover, countries with large welfare states—like Sweden—have high rates of innovation. Stockholm is known as the "Silicon Valley" of Europe despite not having the advantages of actual Silicon Valley companies. Stockholm produces a disproportionate share of 'unicorn' companies (companies valued at over $1 billion). These include companies like Skype, Spotify, King Digital, Minecraft-maker Mojang, and Klarna. Nordic countries also have higher employment rates than the US, higher GDP per capita, higher rates of growth in GDP per capita, more triadic patents (those filed simultaneously in the US, EU, and Japan), higher start-up rates than the US, a higher percentage of business expenditure on research and development as a percentage of GDP, and a higher percentage of venture capital as a percent of GDP.[43] Larger welfare states don't seem to hamper innovation. If it did, it wouldn't make any sense. Social welfare programs keep more people healthy and provide them with better education. Both are key ingredients that lead to innovation.

It should also be noted that some on the right claim that countries like Norway can spend so much on social welfare programs because they have huge oil reserves relative to the size of their economy, which act as a sort of natural "gift" that state-owned oil companies can sell in order to generate enough revenue to pay for social programs. Aren't countries like Norway just lucky in this respect? No. It's not just Norway that can afford a robust welfare state, but all Nordic countries.

But aren't these countries small compared to the US, and doesn't their smaller size make it easier for them to administer social-democratic welfare programs? Not at all. If anything, their smaller size should make it harder to have a large welfare state. Smaller countries have less diversified economies and smaller domestic markets. Foreign investors can more easily pass on these countries if their governments implement social-democratic welfare programs (or higher taxes) that investors don't like. Rich people in these countries can move to neighboring countries for the same reason. Their smaller size should *limit* the wealth these countries generate and what they can spend on social welfare programs. Yet somehow this isn't a problem. Smaller populations also make it difficult to take advantage of economies of scale. Once these programs are set up, it's trivially easy to add more beneficiaries. If anything, the size of the US should make administering these policies more efficient and reduce the amount of social spending per capita.[44]

Some have argued that a stronger welfare state in the US isn't possible on other grounds—because the US isn't "culturally homogeneous," for example. According to the right, those who reside in countries with strong social-democratic welfare programs share similar values. This homogeneity supposedly leads to less disagreement on whether to accept a larger welfare state. But in the US, support for higher taxes on the rich, a higher minimum wage, a single-payer healthcare system, free college, etc. enjoy widespread support, even among a significant fraction of Republicans.[45] The reason we don't implement these programs is because the rich have corrupted our political system and blocked these reforms, not because the reforms lack public support. Furthermore, while there may not be as large of a consensus in the US regarding these policies as there is in countries like Norway or Finland, this is in no small part due to the proliferation of right-wing propaganda meant to convince people not to support such programs. These "cultural" differences are largely manufactured, not some immutable obstacle that can't be overcome.

But don't countries with large welfare states all have small military budgets? Can't they afford to spend more on social welfare programs because they rely on countries like the US to keep the peace? The US doesn't have this luxury, and therefore can't afford to divert resources to social spending, according to the right. This is laughable. The US military budget is notoriously bloated. Indeed, much of our "defense" spending is, at best, a form of corporate welfare indirectly related to national security. Never mind that the US spends more on its military than the next ten countries combined and could, therefore, defend the country with far less spending. But again, this spending is not for actual defense; its purpose is to project US power across the globe to serve the interests of its corporate elite. We spent $2 trillion on the war in Afghanistan, and the only people who benefited were Raytheon and Northrop Grumman stockholders.[46]

But can't we just rely on private charity to solve problems like poverty? Not at all. As economist Mike Konczal has shown, private charity can come nowhere near meeting society's needs. Private charity is notoriously ineffective, especially when it's needed the most, such as during an economic downturn. Only a robust welfare state can meet these needs.[47] What's more is that it would cost relatively little—an additional 1.08 percent of US GDP—to end poverty. The US could easily afford this trivial expenditure.[48]

The truth is that the US could easily build a robust social-democratic welfare state (and all but eliminate poverty) if it weren't prevented from doing so by moneyed interests. The US is by far the wealthiest nation in the world, and other countries have won the battle against poverty with far fewer resources. The US can afford to waste hundreds of billions of dollars on military spending and other corporate handouts, tax expenditures for the affluent that subsidize their retirement, healthcare, mortgages, stock portfolios, inheritances, and so on. When taking private spending into account, the US already pays for the most expensive welfare state in the world. It's just bloated, inefficient, and is set up to primarily benefit the affluent.[49]

When the right says we "can't afford it," they don't mean that we lack enough money to pay for it. They mean the government doesn't generate enough tax revenue to pay for it. But this is only because the rich have intentionally starved the government of revenue by cutting taxes. This is one reason why the US is one of the lowest-taxed countries among the OECD. If we want to pay for a robust social safety net, we could raise taxes on corporate profits, tax all sources of income at the same rate (currently capital gains are taxed less), raise marginal tax rates, create additional tax brackets for the highest incomes, tax financial transactions, institute a modest wealth tax, and add a value-added tax. This would generate more than enough revenue to fund all of the social programs we need.[50]

It's also obvious that the right isn't concerned about increased social spending per se. If they were, they could just reverse the policies they've favored over the past five decades. We could raise the minimum wage, do a better job of enforcing labor laws, regulate the financial industry, enforce antitrust law, institute a higher inflation target (and thereby reduce unemployment), restructure trade agreements to benefit workers, etc. These reforms would allow workers to demand a greater share of the economic pie before taxes, and therefore reduce the need for public transfers. For the right, the real issue isn't public spending.

It's about who has more power—employers or employees, for example—and maintaining economic, social, and political inequality.

But won't the rich just evade taxes if we raise tax rates to pay for a more robust welfare state? This too is a myth. As Emannuel Saez and Gabriel Zucman have shown, the rich can be forced to pay their fair share of taxes by enforcing existing tax law, creating a "Public Protection Bureau" to regulate the tax-dodging industry, outlawing share buybacks (these were illegal before 1982), and eliminating corporate tax loopholes. We could, for example, introduce a minimum tax on corporate profits to negate the benefits of using offshore tax shelters. If we set such a tax rate at 25 percent, and a multinational headquartered in the US were to shift its profits to a tax haven where they pay a lower rate, the US government could collect the difference. This could be enforced by incorporating tax coordination agreements into trade deals, or by leveling sanctions against tax shelters.[51]

Social-democratic welfare programs aren't doomed to fail. They only fail because the right has too much power and does everything they can to undermine—if not sabotage—these programs. Want social-democratic welfare programs to succeed? Take away the right's power.

CHAPTER SIX

Personal Responsibility

The right claims to value "personal responsibility." What this means is that individuals shouldn't blame others, or society, for their own economic situation. If an individual finds themself in a tough economic situation, it's because they make bad choices; if they made better choices, they'd be able to achieve success. Take the so-called legacy of slavery that liberals blame for the extreme racial disparities in income and wealth we see today. According to the right, the "legacy of slavery" story is a cop out. The right wonders how something that happened over 150 years ago can continue to harm such a large percentage of the black population today. Similarly, Jim Crow ended over 50 years ago. Haven't blacks had plenty of time to catch up to whites? The fact that we're so far removed from slavery and Jim Crow, yet blacks still make up a disproportionate share of the poor, must mean something other than slavery or Jim Crow is to blame for the economic situation of impoverished blacks. The answer? "Personal responsibility."

Furthermore, according to the right, even if racial disparities aren't due to a lack of personal responsibility on the part of individual blacks, these disparities *can't* be due to broader societal factors, for example institutional racism; therefore the rest of society has no responsibility to help alleviate racial disparities. Just look at the places where black poverty is the most pronounced. The right loves to point out that it's black, Democratic politicians who run the cities where black poverty is concentrated. If something other than personal responsibility is to blame for the problems poor blacks face, it's *other black people*. If we want to reduce racial inequality we should at least stop pointing the finger at white people i.e. "institutional racism." If black leaders would refrain from implementing wrongheaded policies, the economic obstacles blacks face would be sufficiently reduced. Forcing the rest of society to adopt these policies would only make the problems blacks face worse.

The right is wrong on both of these points. For one, the right is ignorant of what the legacy of slavery and Jim Crow actually means. After Jim Crow was outlawed, blacks continued to face discrimination in housing, education, employment, access to credit, the criminal justice system, the list goes on. More importantly, elites enacted economic policies that kept blacks down. These economic policies weren't created to harm blacks specifically, but disproportionately harm blacks because these policies are meant to disempower the working class—and because blacks make up a disproportionate share of the working class, which of course is a direct result of slavery and Jim Crow. It's silly to claim that personal responsibility is to blame for racial disparities today, given that we're only a few generations removed from Jim Crow, and that the harmful economic policies elites instituted after Jim Crow continue to the present.

Here we see why debates about institutional racism are often unproductive. When we focus narrowly on institutional racism, we ignore other economic policies that have kept blacks down since the end of Jim Crow. Elites have been a waging class war on the rest of society, the effects of which dwarf those of institutional racism. When we lose sight of this, it can seem plausible that factors like personal responsibility may indeed underlie racial disparities because institutional racism—while certainly an ongoing problem—can only partially explain the racial disparities we see today. It also follows that the "solutions" offered by the right, along with liberals, will either do nothing or remain woefully inadequate if we aim to significantly reduce racial inequality.

All for the better if you're among the elite. Fake solutions like doing nothing, or enacting superficial reforms to reduce racial bias, benefit both liberal and right-wing elites, who would love nothing more than for questions of economic justice to recede into the background while they continue to benefit from status quo political and economic institutions. It's also politically advantageous for establishment politicians who, in the right's case can rile up their base of followers by convincing them that "social justice warriors" and their liberal allies in government and the media unfairly label the right as "racist," or in the case of liberal elites, can gain support by claiming to "fight racism" while letting themselves off the hook from instituting substantive reforms that would drastically improve the lives of millions, a disproportionate number of whom are black.

The Legacy of Slavery

The right claims that blacks no longer face economic and political obstacles that hold them back. One of the reasons they offer to support this claim is the fact that slavery ended over 150 years ago. While it was once true that blacks were oppressed by institutions such as slavery, they've had plenty of time to catch up and achieve an acceptable level of economic independence. If they haven't by now, it must be due to something else, namely a lack of personal responsibility. "No evidence-based attempt has been made to prove that living individuals have been adversely affected by a slave system that was ended over 150 years ago," writes right-wing commentator David Horowitz.[1] This view demonstrates a profound ignorance of what the legacy of slavery entails, along with how this legacy continued to affect the lives of black people long after slavery was abolished.

No one claims that slavery *by itself* adversely affects blacks today. From the moment slavery ended, white people began erecting other institutions to disadvantage blacks, and continue to do so. This is what is meant by the "legacy of slavery." After emancipation, for example, blacks occupied land that had been confiscated or abandoned during the Civil War. Having worked the land for years while their masters contributed nothing, former slaves felt they were entitled to own this land. But the government sided with the former masters, refused to acknowledge the freedmen's claims, and took back the land on the masters' behalf.[2] Without land, blacks found themselves subject to new forms of subjugation. All over the South, whites enforced Black Codes—laws that forced blacks into tenancy, sharecropping, and debt peonage. Whites made it illegal to be landless and without a job, forcing blacks into labor contracts or "apprenticeships" with white landowners, under which blacks had to agree to work under conditions that mirrored slavery.[3] Others were literally re-enslaved. Those who strayed from their plantation were arrested by white sheriffs, whipped, charged with crimes, convicted by all-white juries, and leased to corporations as prison laborers.[4]

Efforts to end this system of exploitation were met with massive resistance. The North, for example, occupied the South after the Civil War and established Reconstruction governments throughout the region. These governments gave blacks the right to vote, protected blacks from violence at the hands of racist southern whites, helped establish schools, and supported the Freedmen's Bureau, an organization that aimed to redistribute land and ensure that labor contracts between freedmen and their former masters were fair.[5] However, Reconstruction only lasted until 1877, at which point the North pulled out of the South, allowing white southerners to take back control of their state governments and impose Jim Crow laws. These laws established a system of racial segregation, relegating blacks to inferior schools and public accommodations, thereby limiting their educational and economic opportunities. Whites also used poll taxes, literacy tests, and all-white primaries to prevent blacks from voting, precluding blacks from using the political system to alter the economic and social injustices they faced.[6] Jim Crow wasn't formally abolished until *1965*, a century after emancipation.

Blacks outside the South faced similar circumstances. Those who migrated to northern cities in search of jobs faced employment discrimination and were relegated to the worst industrial jobs or low-paid service work. No matter what jobs they got, they were paid less than their white counterparts.[7] The government also segregated blacks by destroying integrated neighborhoods under the guise of "urban renewal" programs and upholding discriminatory zoning practices that restricted certain neighborhoods to single-family homes blacks couldn't afford. This contributed to overcrowding in "ghettos," which received far less funding for schools and other public goods. Just like in the South, these practices limited access to the same quality of education that whites enjoyed.[8]

Blacks also faced obstacles when attempting to build wealth. Banks often refused to lend money to blacks, preventing them from purchasing a home.[9] For those who were able to save enough money to buy homes, whites created racial covenants (contracts that barred each other from selling to blacks) and resorted to violence to keep blacks out of their neighborhoods.[10] When the Supreme Court ruled that racial covenants couldn't be enforced, whites found ways around the law. Real estate agents, for example, steered blacks away from white neighborhoods.[11] Where it became possible for blacks to move into better neighborhoods, predatory lenders systematically robbed them of their wealth on a massive scale. They instituted "blockbusting" schemes, scaring white residents out of their neighborhoods, buying their houses for next to nothing, then selling the houses to blacks on contract at inflated prices knowing that many were likely to miss a payment. When they did, the banks confiscated the homes and re-sold them over and over again.[12]

As blacks slowly overcame many of these barriers, whites found new ways to screw them over. As blacks migrated to cities, affluent whites, as well as white-owned businesses, moved to the suburbs. This destroyed jobs and reduced funds for public services and education, leaving those who remained in inner cities impoverished.[13] The government subsidized this "white flight," backing home mortgages to whites while building freeways to connect the suburbs to cities.[14] Blacks who *could* afford to move out of the inner cities often did so, leaving the poorest behind.[15]

Government assistance has also disproportionately benefited whites during economic downturns. During the Great Depression, the government instituted New Deal programs that offered people money and jobs. These programs helped blacks a great deal, but excluded agricultural and service workers, a disproportionate number of whom were black. Employment programs like the NRA also paid blacks less than their white counterparts. These government programs helped create a safety net for the expanding white middle class, allowed whites to more easily build wealth, and helped blacks to a large degree, but progress for blacks was limited.[16]

After World War II, blacks continued to face employment discrimination. When wartime production tailed off in the 1940s, blacks were the first to be laid off, and white soldiers returning from the war took the best new jobs.[17] By the time blacks gained full rights in the mid-1960s, many of the well-paying jobs that had been created during the war were no longer available. Manufacturers steadily shifted production to the South in order to take advantage of favorable business conditions, most notably the lack of a unionized workforce.[18] The effect of these economic conditions can't be overstated. Manufacturing jobs, along with higher rates of unionization, had been the primary ladder to the middle class for unskilled white laborers, and to a large degree blacks as well. But as the economy deindustrialized, most of the jobs that became available to blacks were low-paying service jobs that offered little security or long-term economic mobility.

Given this disgraceful history, it's absurd for the right to claim that a large percentage of blacks are no longer the victims of our political and economic system. Without a massive redistribution of wealth based on the same scale and effort once devoted to uplifting whites during the heyday of the labor movement and the Postwar Boom, there's no reason to expect disadvantaged groups to overcome the harsh inequalities and exploitative conditions that have long characterized our economic system. Instead, we get insufficient government programs, cuts to public jobs, a steady erosion of the minimum wage, excess policing and mass incarceration, mounds of student debt, and no mechanism by which a powerful labor movement might emerge to boost the material interests of those trapped at the bottom of America's economic hierarchy. The right can't admit this because doing so would lead to conclusions they don't like. It's much more convenient for the right to deny any problem exists and hope their audience is too ignorant to push back against the right's distorted version of history—or lacks the empathy to question the racist assumptions that underpin the right's "personal responsibility" narrative.

The Legacy of Jim Crow

The right claims that disadvantaged blacks have nothing to complain about. Jim Crow ended over 50 years ago, and we've spent trillions of dollars on social welfare programs to help blacks in the meantime, yet blacks still remain overrepresented among the poor. According to the right, we shouldn't waste more money on social welfare programs, nor raise other peoples' taxes in order to pay for these programs. David Horowitz writes, "Since the passage of the Civil Rights Acts and the advent of the Great Society in 1965, trillions of dollars in transfer payments have been made to African-Americans in the form of welfare benefits and racial preferences (in contracts, job placements and educational admissions). ... If trillion dollar redistributions and wholesale rewriting of American law (in order to accommodate racial preferences) for African-Americans is not enough to achieve 'healing,' what will?"[19] The Civil Rights Act and the money spent on social welfare programs, however, are minuscule relative to the magnitude of the problems blacks have faced over the past five decades.

When Congress passed the Civil Rights Act, segregation didn't all of a sudden go away. Civil rights laws often went unenforced for decades. Rather than integrate their schools, in some places southern whites shut them down and instituted voucher systems that allowed whites to attend all-white private schools. When blacks attempted to attend formerly all-white public schools, whites formed mobs and attacked school buses full of black children.[20] Civil Rights laws also didn't apply to the North, where "de facto" segregation had long existed due to discriminatory zoning laws. The Supreme Court made this problem worse by striking down busing laws that could have integrated northern schools, as well as lower court rulings that called for equal school funding.[21] These laws have yet to change. As a result, segregation has gotten worse over the past three decades, while schools in poor districts remain wildly underfunded compared to schools in more affluent districts. This helps ensure that blacks continue to lack the same quality of education as whites.[22]

Racism also persisted in housing markets, limiting blacks' ability to build wealth. To this day, lenders push blacks into subprime loans at higher rates than whites with the same financial qualifications. One consequence of this form of discrimination was that the 2006 housing crisis disproportionately affected blacks, wiping out the perceived economic gains thought to come with home ownership.[23] In cities, gentrification also causes rents to increase, which disproportionately harms blacks. Rising rent eats up a larger and larger share of their paychecks and limits their ability to save, forcing them to either stay in cities—but with less disposable income—or to move into segregated suburbs.[24] Laws that allow landlords to easily evict their tenants have also had devastating effects—particularly on single, black women—keeping them trapped in poverty.[25] Municipalities have also cut back spending on legal aid to the poor, leaving poor tenants without adequate council when battling their landlords in court.[26]

To blame poor blacks for their own problems, the right has cynically used the fact that many cities where these problems persist have long been run by black, Democratic politicians. Because these leaders are black, and elected with black support, the right says blacks have no one to blame but themselves (or at least other blacks). The fact that these cities are run by black Democrats, however, doesn't mean that poor blacks are to blame for the conditions they face. These politicians don't represent the interests of their poor constituents, but the interests of their own social class and those of their political donors. As author Keeanga-Yamahtta Taylor has shown, most of them come from the ranks of the professional class and the business establishment, share the interests and values of these constituencies, and receive financial backing from these sectors. While these politicians often use radical rhetoric to appeal to the poor, they're often more interested in promoting "black capitalism" than enacting a progressive economic agenda. Indeed, it's advantageous for business interests to support black politicians in many cases because these figures can use their "blackness" as cover to scold poor blacks about their lack of "personal responsibility" in a way that whites can't. Once elected to office, these candidates then build political machines to entrench their power and crush any opposition, which includes the left.[27]

It's also important to understand the context in which black leaders came to power in American cities. Black mayors began to win elections during a time of economic stagnation, deindustrialization, and white flight, which deprived cities of tax revenue which might have otherwise been used to invest in black communities. Buildings crumbled and residents had little incentive, nor the financial means, to improve their neighborhoods and build wealth.[28] The federal government also contributed to these problems by diverting funding meant for community programs into policing under the guise of a "war on crime" and a "war on drugs" during the Nixon and Reagan administrations. These policies continue to this day. Indeed, politicians from both parties understand it's cheaper to pay for a draconian carceral state rather than provide a robust social safety net for individuals in impoverished communities.[29] Other programs, such as food stamps, welfare, unemployment insurance, and school lunch programs, have been continually slashed since the 1970s, along with funding for hundreds of thousands of public sector jobs that had once been the primary means for blacks to enter the middle class.[30]

Both the Democratic and Republican parties have supported these policies. Bill Clinton, for example, signed the 1996 "welfare reform" bill into law, which gutted assistance to single mothers.[31] These policies reflected a rightward shift within the Democratic Party that began in the 1980s, and were part of a broader economic agenda known as neoliberalism. Other pillars of this agenda include making it easier for companies to bust unions, trade agreements that let corporations offshore jobs, tight monetary policy that generates unemployment, and letting the minimum wage erode, each of which weakens the bargaining power of workers, undermining the mechanism by which they might be able to move up the income ladder. All of these policies create poverty on an ongoing basis—and have more or less remained in place to this day.[32]

Racial bias also continues to pervade every level of America's criminal justice system. Police stop blacks more often than whites, arrest blacks at higher rates than whites, charge them with harsher crimes than whites, convict them with greater frequency than whites, and sentence them more severely than whites, all *for the same infractions committed by whites*. Those who are convicted of more severe crimes are often stripped of their right to vote, as well as access to public services, and must label themselves as felons on job applications when they get out of jail, making them all but unemployable.[33] This increases recidivism, since many have few options other than to commit "survival crimes," making them more likely to get swept back up into the criminal justice system—especially given the prevalence of draconian "three strikes" laws, which automatically send convicted felons back to jail for even minor offenses.[34] These policies destroy the lives of the incarcerated, as well as their families, and have devastated black communities.

Blacks also continue to face obstacles built into our political system. The Electoral College—literally a legacy of slavery—reduces the political power of black voters on average, since it gives disproportionate representation to Republican-leaning states that favor policies aimed at hurting the poor. Republicans have also used a number of voter suppression tactics to disenfranchise poor voters. These include voter ID laws, voter caging, purging voter rolls, limiting early voting, limiting polling places in locations that lean Democratic, preventing same-day voter registration, and using the police to deter blacks from voting.[35] Conservative majorities on the Supreme Court have made these problems worse by opening the floodgates to unlimited corporate spending on political campaigns. Corporate spending helps elect right-wing politicians to Congress, who favor policies that give more power to the rich, and therefore take power away from the poor—again, a disproportionate number of whom are black.[36]

It's silly to claim that blacks no longer face obstacles because we passed civil rights laws in the 1960s. The right only wants to make it seem this way in order to trick society into accepting policies the right favors, which empowers employers and lets the rich keep more of their wealth.

Institutional Racism

Many on the right deny that institutional racism exists. Right-wing "intellectual" Ben Shapiro claims, "The idea that black people in the

US are disproportionately poor because America is racist; that's just not true, at least not in terms of America's racism today keeping black people down." Shapiro goes on to explain, "I wasn't born when Jim Crow was in place; I wasn't an adult when Jim Crow was in place. I know that I'm not a racist and I know I haven't acted in a racist manner." Shapiro elsewhere denies the existence of institutional racism because no one can show him "specific policies" that exist today that were created with "racist intent."[37] There are a number of problems with Shapiro's take. While there is a kernel of truth to what Shapiro claims, he's wrong to dismiss the effects of institutional racism. And while institutional racism may not be the primary culprit behind the extreme levels of racial inequality that characterize our economic system (the kernel of truth), the conclusions one should draw from this fact are the polar opposite of what people like Ben Shapiro believe, which is that we should do nothing to reduce racial disparities.

Let's first note that institutional racism doesn't refer to institutions that exist today that were created with racist intent. Institutional racism includes the legacy of past injustices, such as slavery, Jim Crow, and housing segregation. It also refers to racial bias among those who occupy powerful positions in society, like lawyers, prosecutors, judges, the police, and politicians. Slavery and Jim Crow cemented blacks at the bottom of American society, and decisions by powerful actors contribute to significant disparities in income and wealth, higher incarceration rates, limited access to the vote, and so on. Note that none of these factors involve institutions that still exist today that were created with racist intent, yet they still harm millions of blacks.

Take slavery and Jim Crow. These institutions no longer exist, but we're only five decades removed from the formal end of Jim Crow. There's no reason to expect blacks to have caught up to whites in such a brief period, given that the parents or grandparents of those living today would have lived under Jim Crow, and as a result may not have been able to provide the same educational opportunities, financial assistance, and so on, to their children when compared to those who didn't suffer under Jim Crow. Or take racial bias in hiring practices. Studies have shown that résumés with "black"-sounding names are less likely than those with "white"-sounding names to receive callbacks from employers even when they have the same qualifications. This form of discrimination limits the ability of blacks to earn incomes at the same level as whites.[38] Or take racial bias in the criminal justice system. Police engage in racial profiling and arrest blacks at higher rates, prosecutors hit blacks with more severe charges, juries convict blacks at higher rates, and judges impose harsher sentences on blacks. These forms of discrimination may only involve implicit bias, yet they destroy the lives of the incarcerated, as well as their families and communities.[39] It's therefore odd to claim that institutional racism doesn't remain a problem in American society (let alone claim that it doesn't exist), or that we have no responsibility to remedy these social ills.

Yet this isn't the whole story. While slavery and Jim Crow certainly placed blacks at the bottom of America's economic hierarchy, and racial discrimination in employment, housing, and the criminal justice system still remains a problem, this doesn't mean these factors are the primary culprit behind the enormous racial disparities we see today. Even if we could end discriminatory practices tomorrow, blacks would still remain overrepresented among the poor, and would likely remain so into the foreseeable future, if not indefinitely. This is because our political and economic institutions remain structured in a way that generates extreme levels of economic inequality. When the government makes it easier for employers to bust unions, uses monetary policy to generate unemployment, enters into trade deals that allow corporations to offshore jobs, refuses to raise the minimum wage, sits idly while state governments attack voting rights, and so on, inequality worsens and it becomes harder for those at the bottom of America's economic system—a disproportionate number of whom are black—to get ahead. There's no reason to think that stamping out institutional racism will alleviate this problem.

If we want to dig even deeper than this, we can. Take one of the essential institutions we value as a society: property rights. One can imagine a scenario where wealth is shared relatively equally throughout society and everyone has enough resources to provide for themselves and their families. Property rights could confer ownership of these resources to individuals, providing them with economic security. But this isn't how property rights function in the US. Because our institutions distribute wealth in a way that *doesn't* ensure everyone has access to enough resources, and this distribution of resources is enforced through property law, property rights are among the institutions that perpetuate economic inequality. Blacks weren't able to acquire property until white people had already appropriated most of it, then used their control over these resources to ensure that new wealth flows mostly to themselves. As a result, a disproportionate number of blacks are left without sufficient resources.

None of this is to say we should abolish private property. Property rights form part of the bedrock of a functioning society. But if we don't want racial disparities in income and wealth to remain embedded in our economic and political system, we might recognize how property rights help perpetuate racial inequality, and create alternate institutions that distribute property in a way that differs from the status quo. For example, we could implement a single-payer healthcare system, enact a Green New Deal, provide free college to everyone, provide parents with a child allowance, enforce labor law in a way that gives more power to workers, create more public housing, drastically raise taxes on the rich, and so on. These policies would reduce economic inequality, provide individuals with the basic resources necessary to thrive, and do far more to close the racial wealth gap than any attempt to eliminate institutional racism.

Here we see why establishment liberals and their supporters often exaggerate the social, economic, and political impact of institutional racism. They don't support policies like Medicare for All or a Green New Deal. These policies hurt their stock portfolios and increase their tax liability. They enrage donors. They would put an entire industry of consultants who get paid to advise Democratic political candidates on how to avoid supporting these policies out of a job. And so on. It's therefore advantageous for liberal elites and other grifters to blame society's problems on racism, brand the right as racist, argue with these "racists" on TV, and then pat themselves on the back for "fighting racism" in order to trick voters into supporting the Democratic Party. In reality, liberal elites are helping to perpetuate the problem, which is social and economic inequality.

Institutional racism isn't the entire reason for racial disparities in the US. While it remains a major problem, the extreme racial disparities we see today persist due to policies that disadvantage the poor more broadly. If our goal is to mitigate racial disparities, we need to place economic justice at the forefront of our demands.

CHAPTER SEVEN

The Party of Lincoln

The American right and their liberal adversaries are engaged in a constant battle over which of them is the "most racist." Battles often center around the history of the Democratic and Republican parties, under which liberals and the right, respectively, have consolidated their political power. Liberals point to the Republican Party's history of dog-whistle racism to pander to racial conservatives in the 1960s and 70s to build their electoral base. According to this narrative, southern whites "switched" to the Republican Party in response to the support for civil rights among liberal Democrats. The right, however, claims these accusations are a cynical attempt by Democrats to undermine the Republican Party and gain a political advantage.

To push back against their liberal adversaries, the right has invented a counter-narrative. The right highlights the early days of the

Republican Party, when the Party could count Abraham Lincoln and Frederick Douglass among its ranks, as well as moderates like Dwight Eisenhower, who enforced school integration in the South in 1957; along with congressional Republicans who supported civil rights legislation in the 1960s. Conversely, the right stresses the Democratic Party's history of racism. The Democratic Party was created in the 1830s and was originally dominated by slave owners, and continued to be the party of the KKK and Jim Crow until the 1960s. A liberal wing emerged within the party in the 1930s, but liberals remained allied with segregationists for decades.

So far, so good. No one disputes that Abraham Lincoln was a Republican, or that the Republican Party helped end slavery, or that Eisenhower sent federal troops to enforce integration, and so on. Nor does anyone dispute the early history of Democratic Party, or deny that liberals allied with segregationists well into the twentieth century. Where the right's argument starts to get weird, however, is when they claim that liberal Democrats continued the Democratic Party's legacy of racism by getting blacks hooked on "welfare." The right points out that Democrats created the New Deal in the 1930s, in addition to Lyndon Johnson's Great Society programs in the 1960s. These programs, according to the right, discourage individual initiative, thereby preventing blacks from uplifting themselves. In contrast, the right claims the Republican Party continues to embody the principles for which earlier Republicans once stood, because it offers "freedom," which is best achieved by leaving individuals free to pull themselves up by their own bootstraps and pursue their interests in the free market, not by accepting handouts from Democratic politicians.

Furthermore, the right claims that southern whites *couldn't* have switched to the Republican Party in reaction to liberal Democrats' support for civil rights, because whites left the Democratic Party in the late 80s and early 90s—well after the civil rights era had ended. While some Republicans may have attempted to recruit disaffected Democrats by exploiting racial resentment in the 1960s, this had little effect, if any. Instead, the Republican Party supposedly became competitive in the South due to "economic considerations." When the South's economy grew during the second half of the twentieth century, many individuals earned more income, and this supposedly led to increasing support among southerners who favored conservative economic policies. In contrast, the racist southern Democrats tended to be poor, and remained in the Democratic Party, according to the right. Some on the right even claim that Martin Luther King would be a Republican if he were alive today, for these reasons.

There are a number of problems with the right's story. The right ignores that the Republican Party abandoned civil rights within a decade of emancipation, turned itself into the party of big business, and has more or less remained so ever since. They also ignore that Democratic support for civil rights began in the 1930s, not the 1960s, making the fact that blacks started accepting "handouts" in the 1930s less salient to the right's argument. The claim that a higher percentage of Republicans supported the civil rights bills of the 1960s is also a red herring. Liberal Democrats outnumbered Republicans, and it was liberals who pushed for the major civil rights bills. The Republicans who supported these bills also came primarily from the Republican Party's liberal wing, not its conservative wing.

Nor is it true that white voters in the South waited until the late 1980s to ditch the Democratic Party. They started ditching it in 1948 when liberals within the Democratic Party signaled support for civil rights; then began ditching it at higher rates in the 1960s after President Kennedy gave a nationally-televised speech calling for civil rights legislation. It's also without question that the Republican Party used dog-whistle racism to help build their electoral base in the South, and that Republicans believed this tactic central to their electoral strategy.

A number of factors complicated this process—longstanding Democratic Party entrenchment in the South, strong incentives for southern politicians to remain in the Party, as well as the fact that the Republican Party also counted liberals who supported civil rights among its ranks. These factors precluded the switch from being immediate (notwithstanding the 1964 presidential election). When southern whites began identifying as Republican in the 1980s, it was also due to other factors, including the Republican Party's politicization of issues like abortion. But we have hard data to show that it is indeed these voters—particularly whites in the Deep South, where slavery was most prevalent—who are both more likely to vote Republican and more likely to harbor negative feelings towards blacks.

The idea that "economic considerations" explain the white switch is another red herring. Economic considerations have long served as the basis of an alliance between economic and racial conservatives, and racial and economic issues have always been intertwined. Because racist institutions like slavery and Jim Crow relegated blacks to the bottom of America's economic hierarchy, racial and economic issues can't be easily separated. Indeed, right-wing operatives like Lee Atwater were explicit that "economic" rhetoric made appeals to overt racism superfluous when the Republican Party targeted white voters.

The right's claim that Martin Luther King would be a Republican today is also fraught with problems, to say the least. King witnessed the first seeds of the modern Republican Party take root while he was still alive—and he was far from impressed. Had King lived, he would have seen the Republican Party mutate into a deformed caricature of itself. The Party would follow in the footsteps of segregationists by disenfranchising poor (disproportionately black) voters, push an extreme economic agenda that disproportionately harms people of color, support policies that fuel mass incarceration, and eventually back a corrupt, race-baiting demagogue for President, who reminded many of segregationist George Wallace. While it's far from certain King would support the modern Democratic Party—which hides behind its support for social justice to mask its lack of support for economic justice—the Republican Party remains the primary obstacle to overcoming the problems disadvantaged blacks face today.

The Party of Civil Rights

The right claims that the Republican Party is the party of civil rights, and always has been. The Republican Party was created as an anti-slavery party in the 1850s. Abraham Lincoln was a Republican. So was Frederick Douglass. Republican President Dwight Eisenhower enforced school integration in the 1950s. When Congress passed civil rights laws in the 1960s, it did so with higher support among Republicans than Democrats. The right cites these examples to push back against those who accuse Republicans of sowing racial division and supporting policies that reinforce racial inequality. The right's history of the Republican Party, however, is selective to say the least.

It's true that the Republican Party could once claim to be the party of civil rights. After defeating the South in the Civil War and emancipating the South's slaves, the Republican-led North used military force to occupy the South, give blacks the right to vote, and protect blacks from violence at the hands of racist southern whites. Reconstruction governments in the South also helped build schools and supported the Freedmen's Bureau, an organization that aimed to redistribute land and ensure that labor contracts between freedmen and their former masters were fair. The Bureau often failed to fulfill its duties, as most of these contracts were anything but fair, but Reconstruction was better than the alternative, as it limited the extent to which former masters could re-establish slave-like conditions throughout the region.

Republican efforts to protect the rights of blacks were short lived, however. Republicans colluded with Democrats to end Reconstruction in 1876 when Democrats threatened to contest a close presidential election that year. Republicans negotiated a deal to end Reconstruction if the Democrats backed down, selling out blacks to maintain their political power.[1] Many Republicans also adopted some of the worst attitudes of racist Democrats and so-called Liberal Republicans who had always opposed Reconstruction. They branded blacks and northern workers alike as lazy socialists who wanted to redistribute wealth.[2] Instead of helping blacks, the Republican Party shifted its focus to fighting government regulations, supporting tariff subsidies, mobilizing the military to suppress labor unrest, lobbying for the gold standard, and blocking anti-trust legislation.[3] Moderate Republicans complained that the Party had been consumed by a greed that "has never been surpassed in our political history."[4] Some began to flee the Party, which had become "an organization of political corruption."[5] Teddy Roosevelt lamented that Republican leaders had "permitted themselves to fossilize," and were becoming "ultra-conservative reactionaries" who "oppose all progress."[6]

These ultra-conservative reactionaries would gain control of the Republican Party—and the federal government—in 1920 and preside over a decade of rampant Wall Street speculation and soaring economic inequality while doing nothing to help blacks. This era also saw a resurgence of the KKK, this time in Republican strongholds such as Indiana.[7] The 1920s of course ended with a major stock market crash, followed by a series of bank runs, resulting in the Great Depression.

The Republican Party offered no solutions, instead insisting that recovery would ensue only if we ceded more power to business.[8] As a result, Democrats swept into office and passed the New Deal, and the Republican Party was marginalized for decades.

By the 1960s, the Republican Party was largely made up of moderates and liberals who had come to accept much of the New Deal. These Republicans would have been considered what the modern right now refer to as RINOs (Republicans in Name Only). The right's claim that the civil rights laws of the 1960s enjoyed greater support among Republicans than Democrats is therefore misleading. Not only were these Republicans moderates, but they were small in number compared to Democrats, and acted as junior partners with liberals within the Democratic Party when passing civil rights legislation. Records of House floor speeches, as well as discharge petitions meant to bring the major civil rights bills up for consideration, show these bills originated from liberal Democrats, not Republicans.[9] Democrats even had to weaken the 1964 Civil Rights Act in order to secure Republican support.[10]

Some on the Republican Party's right wing also opposed the Civil Rights Act as part of a new strategy to pick up southern white voters who were leaving the Democratic Party (due to its national leaders' support for civil rights). Republican presidential candidate Barry Goldwater opposed the 1964 Civil Rights Act, and mixed economic rhetoric with racist dog-whistles in order to pander to these potential converts.[11] This marked the acceleration of a party re-alignment under which liberals would consolidate their ranks under the Democratic Party, while conservatives did the same under the Republican Party. Both parties continued to support economic policies that deprived the poor of resources, and thereby helped keep blacks cemented at the bottom of America's economic hierarchy, but the Republican Party supported an even harsher version of this economic agenda.

In addition to the Republican Party's callous economic policies, the Nixon administration's "law and order" politics of the late 1960s and early 1970s set the stage for mass incarceration. Rather than providing the poor with resources to deal with social problems rooted in poverty and institutional racism, the government invested in policing and prisons—a practice that continues to this day.[12] This disproportionately harms blacks, who are more likely to be targeted by the police, more likely to be arrested, more likely to be charged with harsher crimes, less likely to be able to afford adequate legal counsel, more likely to be pressured into accepting plea deals, more likely to be convicted, and more likely to be hit with harsher sentences than whites found guilty of the same crimes.[13]

While "law and order" politics was taking hold, the Supreme Court was shifting to the right and preventing economic progress for blacks. The Court halted school integration and denied equal funding for public schools. These rulings disproportionately harmed blacks, since blacks are more likely to reside in districts with lower levels of funding for education.[14]

Republicans have also sought to limit access to the vote. They've promoted voter ID laws, voter caging, voter roll purges, and felon disenfranchisement laws; reduced polling places in economically disadvantaged voting districts; and gerrymandered their way to an average of 16-17 extra seats in the House of Representatives over the last decade.[15] A conservative majority on the Supreme Court also overturned Section 5 of the Voting Rights Act, allowing states to alter voting laws without federal approval, leading to a slew of voter ID laws and voter roll purges. The point is to reduce Democratic turnout, which disproportionately harms blacks, since blacks are more likely to vote Democrat.[16]

The Republican Party isn't the party of civil rights, and hasn't been for over a century. When the right cites examples of Republican support for civil rights, they're attempting to whitewash the racist parts of the Republican Party's history, as well as mask how the right's pro-business agenda continues to disproportionately harm people of color.

The Black Switch

Right-wing "intellectual" Dinesh D'Souza points out that blacks began voting Democrat following the New Deal, which provided economic relief in the wake of the Great Depression. Blacks supported the Democratic Party even though it was known as the party of slavery, the KKK, and segregation. Rather than reject the Democratic Party's racism, pull themselves up by their own bootstraps, and vote Republican, the right says blacks chose to live on the dole and accept "handouts" from their new Democratic masters, who would keep blacks "enslaved" on a "liberal plantation" of welfare dependency, a problem made worse by Lyndon Johnson's Great Society programs in the 1960s.

The fact that blacks began switching parties during the New Deal, however, doesn't show that blacks vote Democrat to get free stuff. By the mid-1930s, the Republican Party had long abandoned its support for civil rights, destroyed the economy, and refused to offer solutions in response to the economic destruction wrought by the Great Depression.[17] In contrast, liberal Democrats enacted the New Deal, and helped out-of-work Americans by creating the Works Progress Administration, the Civilian Conservation Corps, and the National Youth Administration, which hired hundreds of thousands of black workers. To the extent blacks benefited from the New Deal, it was primarily from these organizations, not "free stuff" they received for doing nothing.[18]

Furthermore, the idea that blacks get free stuff from voting Democrat, whereas whites *don't* get free stuff from voting Republican, is ludicrous. Blacks were enslaved 200 years and subject to Jim Crow laws for another 100 years. During this time, white people were able to accumulate "stuff" while blacks couldn't. Whites couldn't have done this without the help of the government—by clearing the land of America's indigenous inhabitants, giving away cheap land to white settlers, fostering economic development on behalf of white-owned corporations, selectively enforcing the rights of white people, underpinning the distribution of power throughout society by enforcing property rights and unfair employment contracts, the list goes on. Within this system, those with more power use their control over society's resources to exploit those with less, funneling yet more of society's wealth to themselves. Voting Republican both strengthens the power of these (disproportionately white) actors to exploit—by cutting social welfare programs, allowing the minimum wage to erode, using monetary policy to generate unemployment, off-shoring jobs, or refusing to enforce labor laws—and allows whites to keep more of the stuff they're able to accumulate under this arrangement by reducing their taxes and deregulating industry.[19]

But there was another major reason blacks switched to the Democratic Party. Liberals within the Democratic Party began supporting civil rights around the same time they enacted the New Deal. By this time, millions of blacks had migrated to the North in search of manufacturing jobs. As they joined the ranks of the industrial working class, the Congress of Industrial Organizations (CIO)—which was becoming prominent within the Democratic Party at the time—folded many blacks into its ranks. In order to maintain the support of these new members, the CIO pushed the Democratic Party in the North to include civil rights measures in their state party platforms.[20] Within a decade, support for civil rights began to make its way into the Democratic Party's national platform as well. In 1947 President Truman called for anti-lynching laws, ending employment discrimination, and desegregating public facilities. In 1948 Truman integrated the military. Later that year at the Democratic National Convention, Hubert Humphrey called on the Democratic Party to support civil rights.[21] Liberal Democrats would then go on to push for the major civil rights bills of the 1960s.[22] It should come as no surprise that blacks of all income levels overwhelmingly vote Democrat, not just those who benefit from social welfare programs, and have done so since the early 1960s—before Lyndon Johnson's Great Society programs.[23]

This doesn't mean that the modern Democratic Party hasn't failed black communities in many ways. Just like Republicans, Democrats support economic policies that perpetuate structural inequality, which disproportionately harms blacks. Sometimes Democratic politicians—for example, Bill and Hillary Clinton, along with Joe Biden—have painted blacks as violent criminals. Democrats have also supported harsh criminal justice policies that have destroyed black communities. They've engaged in voter suppression in Democratic primaries to ensure that establishment candidates have an advantage over those with more redistributive platforms that would disproportionately help blacks. And they've stood by idly while Republicans take measures to disenfranchise the poor, a disproportionate number of whom are black. Democrats could easily overcome the right's efforts by nuking the Senate filibuster, then passing a modern Civil Rights Act. They just refuse to do so.

But it's one thing to point out these problems with the Democratic Party, and another to defend the Republican Party, which supports *the worst policies of Democrats*, along with a host of even more harmful ones. This is especially true given that the Democratic and Republican parties are the *only two choices we have*, due to America's two-party, winner-take-all electoral system. Blacks have little choice but to accept the lesser of two evils.

Blacks didn't switch parties to get free stuff. They switched because they had little choice, and because Republicans are so *awful* when it comes to racial and economic issues—even worse than the Democratic Party. The right's "black switch" narrative is meant to obscure this reality and trick society into believing that poor people are lazy, and therefore that there's nothing wrong with the current economic system or the inequality it generates. This way the rich can keep more of their wealth, and we can continue funneling money into their pockets.

The White Switch

Over the latter half of the twentieth century, support for the Republican Party in the South grew due to increasing support among conservative whites. Liberals claim conservatives switched from the Democratic Party to the Republican Party in reaction to the Democratic Party's support for civil rights. The right claims this couldn't be true, since the switch took place well after the civil rights era. "If southern rednecks ditched the Democrats because of a civil rights law passed in 1964, it is strange that they waited until the late 1980s and early 1990s to do so," writes right-wing columnist Kevin Williamson.[24]

Contrary to what Williamson claims, however, southern rednecks didn't start ditching the Democratic Party in the late 1980s. They began ditching the Party in 1948, after Democratic President Harry Truman integrated the military, and party leaders like Hubert Humphrey called for the Party to support civil rights.[25] Democratic Senator Strom Thurmond led a faction of segregationist "Dixiecrats" to secede from the party for this reason.[26] After President Kennedy's 1963 speech in support of civil rights, voters left in greater numbers, at which point Republicans began trying to convert them.[27]

The right attempted to appeal to southern whites by using dog-whistle racism. To oppose desegregation, Republicans claimed to favor "states' rights." To oppose busing, Republicans claimed to favor "school choice." To oppose social welfare programs, Republicans branded the beneficiaries of these programs as "welfare queens" who lack "personal responsibility." To oppose higher levels of taxation needed to pay for social welfare programs, Republicans claimed to defend "property rights." To quash dissent among blacks who suffered under America's racist political and economic system, Republicans claimed to support "law and order."[28]

In order to make inroads to the South, however, Republicans had to fight a century-and-a-half of Democratic entrenchment in the region. The Democratic Party had enjoyed almost complete control of southern political institutions since the 1850s. Because the Republican Party initially challenged the social and economic system that existed in the South, Republicans had little chance to succeed in the region. The Republican-led North would go on to destroy the South in the Civil War, free the South's slaves, and occupy the South during Reconstruction. This fueled widespread resentment of the Republican Party. This resentment persisted long after Reconstruction, and was further cemented when the Republican Party destroyed the economy in the late 1920s and early 1930s. By the time the civil rights movement gained steam in the 1950s, 78 percent of southern voters still identified as Democrat and only 9 percent as Republican.[29] This gave the Democratic Party an enormous advantage. Democrats benefited from incumbency, were far more experienced in southern politics, and could neutralize Republican challengers by touting their "conservatism," while disassociating themselves from national Democrats.[30]

When Republicans didn't face these obstacles, the white switch was immediate. In the 1964 presidential election, the choice was limited to Republican Senator Barry Goldwater, who opposed the Civil Rights Act, and Democrat Lyndon Johnson, who was instrumental in passing the Act. When the election took place, the Deep South, and *only* the Deep South, delivered electoral college delegates to Goldwater. These voters would go on to split their votes between segregationist George Wallace and Richard Nixon in 1968 (polls found that 80 percent of Wallace voters preferred Nixon to liberal Democrat Hubert Humphrey that year), then support Nixon by a three to one margin in 1972.[31]

Conservative commentator Mark Levin has offered a novel explanation to show that Republicans couldn't have made gains in the South due to racist attitudes among those who switched. Levin points out that in the years immediately following the major civil rights bills, Republicans could initially make congressional gains only at the southern periphery, in states like Tennessee and North Carolina, rather than Deep South states. Levin claims that because racism was less pronounced in these peripheral states, where the Republican Party enjoyed more support, the Republican Party must be less racist than the Democratic Party.[32] But Levin can only make this claim because he ignores the 1964, 1968, and 1972 presidential elections, and because he limits his time frame for congressional support to the years immediately following passage of the major civil rights bills. During this time, Republicans failed to make congressional gains in the Deep South because this is where the Democratic Party had become, up to that point, the most firmly entrenched. We can therefore get a better idea of what happened in the South if we jump ahead further in time. When we do this, we can see that among southern whites, it's those who live in the Deep South who are the most conservative, the most likely to vote Republican, and the most likely to have negative feelings towards blacks.[33]

The evidence also belies a possible explanation for these conservatives' negative feelings towards blacks, which is that conservative whites just resent poor people, among which blacks just happen to be overrepresented. This can't be true. Whereas blacks in the Deep South were once poorer than those in the rest of the South, economic outcomes between the two areas have been equalized by federal legislation, such as the Civil Rights Act and the Voting Rights Act; yet anti-black attitudes still remain higher in the Deep South among whites who are more likely to be conservative Republicans.[34]

This evidence also puts to rest an argument—made by right-wing commentator Dinesh D'Souza—which posits that the South flipped due to an influx of middle-class professionals who, wanting to keep more of their income, were more likely to support conservative economic policies.[35] For D'Souza's argument to make sense, there would had to have been an out-migration of whites who held positive views towards blacks, or a disproportionate influx of white, middle-class professionals who held negative feelings towards blacks (or some combination of the two), into the Deep South. There's no reason why this should have occurred, and no evidence that it did.[36]

Do we really need detailed evidence to tell us this? After all, it's not liberal Democrats who defend statues of former Confederate generals, nor proudly wave Confederate flags in defense of "states' rights," nor constantly denigrate blacks as lazy welfare bums and thugs. The people who do this overwhelmingly vote Republican. This doesn't mean that the emergence of the Republican Party in the South was *solely* due to racism, or that all southern Republicans are individually racist. Nor does it mean that the Democratic Party hasn't exploited the modern Republican Party's racist roots in a cynical manner in order to gain a political advantage. But if we want to understand the history of our two major political parties, the data (as well as common sense) shows the switch took place.

Dog-Whistle Racism

Many on the right deny that dog-whistle racism played a major role in building the Republican Party's electoral base in the South. "There is no question that Republicans in the 1960s and thereafter hoped to pick up the angry populists who had delivered several states to [Alabama Governor George] Wallace," right-wing commentator Kevin Williamson claims, "But in the main they did not do so by appeal to racial resentment, direct or indirect."[37] Conservative intellectual Dinesh D'Souza wonders if Republicans used dog-whistle racism at all. "Progressives insist that Nixon made a racist 'dog whistle' appeal to Deep South voters. Evidently he spoke to them in a kind of code. Really?" he asks.[38] It's without question, however, that the Republican Party's use of dog-whistle racism played a major role in establishing the Republican Party's electoral base in the South.

Dog-whistle racism is one of the primary reasons Republicans could start to campaign in the South after a century of nearly unchallenged Democratic Party rule. In the decades leading up to 1952, the Republican Party made little effort to win support in the South, having faced widespread resentment in the region dating back to the Civil War and Reconstruction. This began to change, however, when the Party revealed its 1952 presidential platform, which reversed the Party's prior support for federal action against employment discrimination. The Party's new "states' rights" stance on this issue allowed Dwight Eisenhower to compete in much of the South that year.

After winning the presidency, Eisenhower helped the Republican Party build a permanent organizational base throughout the South, which he hoped would promote a moderate brand of conservatism in the region. But the party infrastructure Eisenhower helped create was soon taken over by extremists who would go on to support Arizona Senator Barry Goldwater, a pro-business conservative who mixed economic and racial rhetoric in order to appeal to both economic and racial conservatives, while hiding behind the veneer of plausible deniability dog-whistle racism offers.[39]

Goldwater himself was not an extremist on racial issues, but he understood he could gain support in the South by supporting the same policies as segregationists. He criticized the Supreme Court for its decision in *Brown v. Board of Education*, as well as President Eisenhower for sending troops to enforce *Brown*, and opposed the 1964 Civil Rights Act.[40] Goldwater was careful to couch his views in terms of opposition to government overreach rather than an outright defense of segregation. In 1960 he told southern voters, "There's hardly enough difference between Republican conservatives and the Southern Democrats to put a piece of paper between," and in a 1961 speech that he would "bend every muscle [he had] to see that the South has a voice on everything that affects the life of the South."[41] Goldwater also allied himself with pro-business conservatives like South Carolina Senator Strom Thurmond. "I know this isn't customary for a Republican," Goldwater explained, "but I just wish to God we could find some more Strom Thurmonds in this country."[42] Thurmond was not just a pro-business conservative, however. He also happened to be one of the most ardent segregationists in Congress. That's why it wasn't "customary" to praise him.

The aim of Goldwater's strategy was obvious at the time. Moderate and liberal Republicans questioned whether the GOP should "trade Lincoln for Strom Thurmond."[43] Others in the Party worried that Goldwater was turning the GOP into the "white man's party,"[44] and observed that southern Republicans were trying to "outsegregate the segregationists."[45] This didn't bother Goldwater's backers, who openly called for the Republican Party to "forget all the sentimental tradition of the party of Lincoln," because it "might work wonders in attracting white Southerners into the Republican Party."[46] Goldwater himself even had a name for this strategy. He called it "hunting where the ducks are."[47]

Goldwater was routed in 1964 because of his association with segregationists. But other Republicans realized they could succeed if they used a moderate version of Goldwater's tactics. Richard Nixon claimed to support civil rights and distanced himself from Goldwater, but also assured southern GOP leaders he would do the bare minimum to enforce civil rights legislation in exchange for their support.[48] Nixon also used Thurmond as a proxy, enlisting Thurmond to campaign for him in the South, which became Nixon's largest base of support.[49] This led supporters of segregationist George Wallace to angrily accuse Thurmond of "splitting the white vote."[50] These voters would go on to support Nixon in 1972 by a three to one margin.[51] Nixon would also brand himself as the "law and order" candidate against a backdrop of social unrest in cities throughout the country.[52]

Those close to Nixon have explained the aim of Nixon's strategy. White House Chief of Staff H.R. Halderman wrote in his diary that Nixon "emphasized that you have to face the fact that the whole problem is really the blacks. The key is to devise a system that recognized this while not appearing to."[53] Nixon's special counsel John Ehrlichman also recalled, "We'll go after the racists." According to Ehrlichman, the "subliminal appeal to the anti-black voter was always present in Nixon's statements and speeches."[54] Nixon himself even said of one of his campaign commercials, "Yep, this hits it right on the nose … it's all about law and order and the damn Negro-Puerto Rican groups out there."[55]

Conservative presidential candidates have continued to use these tactics ever since. Ronald Reagan branded himself as the "law and order" candidate when running for governor of California in the wake of the 1964 Watts riots, and opposed the state's Fair Housing Act.[56] In his 1976 presidential bid, he fabricated stories of "welfare queens" in order to stoke racial resentment and gain support among conservative whites.[57] He also launched his 1980 presidential campaign in Philadelphia, Mississippi, where three civil rights activists had been murdered in 1964, and claimed to support "states' rights." Reagan was widely criticized for using these tactics.[58] George H. W. Bush used the same playbook, winning the presidency in 1988 due largely to his campaign's racist "Willie Horton" ad, which claimed that Bush's opponent Michael Dukakis was letting black rapists out of prison. The man behind the ad was Lee Atwater, who'd used similar tactics when he worked for Strom Thurmond decades earlier.[59]

This embarrassing history led some Republicans to admit their wrongs. In 2005, RNC chairman Ken Mehlman admitted, "Some Republicans gave up on winning the African American vote, looking the other way or trying to benefit politically from racial polarization. I am here today as the Republican chairman to tell you we were wrong."[60] But this didn't stop Donald Trump from peddling deranged "birther" conspiracies meant to delegitimize Barack Obama's presidential candidacy by claiming he is not in fact a US citizen, or from scapegoating "illegal immigrants," which Trump claimed were criminals and rapists, or from echoing Nixon's calls for "law and order" in opposition to Black Lives Matter protests. While the nature of dog-whistle racism prevents us from measuring its effects with a great deal of precision, this shouldn't prevent us from calling out the right's history of exploiting racism. Nor should we allow Republicans to gain support for their reactionary agenda by hiding behind the thin veneer of plausible deniability their supposedly race-neutral rhetoric offers.

Economic Considerations

According to the right, the Republican Party became competitive in the once-solid Democratic South not due to a racist backlash among conservative whites, but because of "economic considerations." The right claims that as the South developed economically and incomes rose, it became more middle class. In turn, Southern conservatism became rooted in support for lower taxes and fewer regulations, as well as anti-communism. "Economic considerations" and anti-communism, however, have long served as a potential basis for economic and racial conservatives to form cross-party alliances, and eventually helped the right bring racial conservatives into the Republican Party.

Economic considerations have united economic and racial conservatives since the 1870s. After the Civil War, businessmen in the Republican Party saw opportunities to enrich themselves by rebuilding the South's economy. They viewed northern intervention during Reconstruction as a hurdle to economic development, attacked such intervention as "socialism" and "communism," and portrayed the beneficiaries of this intervention as lazy welfare bums.[61] The Republican Party then ended Reconstruction and transformed itself into the party of big business, at which point Republican support among blacks began to deteriorate. By the 1930s, the GOP had "lost the Negro vote," according to some within the party leadership, and therefore became "determined to go after the South."[62] Economic considerations formed the basis of this potential alliance. After Franklin Roosevelt routed Republican Alf Landon in the 1936 presidential election, Republicans began exploring the possibility of creating a coalition ticket to defeat liberals like Roosevelt, hoping southern Democrats who opposed the incorporation of organized labor within the Democratic Party would join them.[63] At the 1938 Alabama state GOP convention, RNC Chairman John Hamilton attempted to forge this new alliance. Hamilton told Republican supporters that there's "no insurmountable barrier between the real Democrats of the South and the Republican party." The only reason such a barrier existed, according to Hamilton, was because "deep-seated loyalty that comes from years of loving and serving their party keeps many southern Democrats today from formally and openly repudiating it under its present leadership."[64] Author Elizabeth McRae has likewise shown how politically active elites in the South during this period attempted to forge connections with conservative business interests and the Republican Party outside of the South, while assuring skeptical whites that such an alliance wouldn't undermine segregation and white supremacy.[65] Republicans and southern Democrats would also partner on anti-labor legislation, such as the Smith-Connally Act in 1943 and the Taft-Hartley Act in 1947.

Despite these connections, opportunities for a full-blown political realignment remained limited. Southern segregationists benefited more from an alliance with liberal Democrats. They gained from New Deal economic reforms, as well as large Democratic majorities in Congress, which allowed them to procure pork-barrel spending for their home districts. Segregationists also constituted a large enough voting bloc to filibuster civil rights legislation. They had the best of both worlds.

An emerging rift between segregationists and liberals within the Democratic Party, however, would provide new opportunities for business interests within the Republican Party to ally with segregationist Democrats and begin to build an electoral base in the South. Strom Thurmond, a pro-business conservative and a segregationist whose opponents often accused him of being the puppet of wealthy businessmen, led the 1948 Dixiecrat revolt in response to support for civil rights among liberal Democrats. RNC Chairman Guy Gabrielson attempted to court these Dixiecrats to create a "unity ticket." One of the reasons Gabrielson offered was that "the Dixiecrat party believes in states' rights. That's what the Republican Party believes in."⁶⁶ House Republican Karl Mundt likewise tried to convert Democratic voters to the Republican cause, explaining, "Their viewpoint is similar, their fears are similar. They both stand against an overpowerful central government, and for maintenance of local and state responsibilities." Mundt believed that "the South is the natural and logical source of new strength for the Republican party," and that a potential coalition between southern conservatives and Republicans would be based on a "strong political kinship."⁶⁷

Despite this strong political kinship, Republicans had long struggled to make inroads to the South. As Hamilton noted in 1938, Democratic Party entrenchment precluded a strong Republican presence in the region. But this changed once the Republican Party began to back off its support for civil rights. In 1952, the Republican Party waffled on its support for the Fair Employment Practice Committee, which had been established to prevent discrimination in government jobs. Republican opposition to the FEPC allowed Dwight Eisenhower to campaign in the South, and later build a permanent organizational base in the region, which would be taken over by far right elements within the Party who aimed to court southern whites.⁶⁸

Economic considerations played an important role in this strategy. Former Reagan advisor Lee Atwater explains, "You start out in 1954 by saying, 'Nigger, nigger, nigger.' By 1968 you can't say 'nigger'—that hurts you, backfires. So you say stuff like, uh, forced busing, states' rights, and all that stuff, and you're getting so abstract. Now, you're talking about cutting taxes, and all these things you're talking about are totally economic things and a byproduct of them is, blacks get hurt worse than whites."⁶⁹ In other words, the Republican Party didn't need to oppose blacks having access to a quality education; they could oppose "forced busing" and support "states' rights." They didn't need to oppose blacks having access to public accommodations; they could support "property rights." They didn't need to oppose blacks having economic security; they could oppose higher levels of taxation needed to pay for social welfare programs. In other words, the "economic" policies they supported functioned to maintain a system of racial inequality without having to appeal to overtly racist attitudes among racial conservatives.

The relationship between economic considerations and opposition to civil rights was symbiotic. Author Nancy McClean has documented how right-wing economists like James Buchanan piggybacked on the public backlash among segregationists to peddle crank economic theories meant to justify the right's economic agenda. Buchanan played off of segregationists' opposition to federal intervention on racial matters, which helped popularize the idea that government officials are inherently corrupt and therefore incapable of helping the broader public (for example, by instituting social welfare programs). These ideas have been used by conservative intellectuals and politicians ever since to gain support for lower taxes, privatization, and deregulation.[70]

The right's attempt to isolate "economic considerations" as the sole factor in the shift among southern whites towards the Republican Party masks a long history of exploiting racial conservatism. Republicans used "economic" rhetoric to help consolidate economic and racial conservatives into the Party's electoral base, help the Party gain political power, and enact economic policies that primarily benefit the rich.

The Conservative Dr. King

Many on the right claim that if Martin Luther King were still alive, he would be a conservative, if not a Republican. According to the right,

King would never support the types of policies advocated by so-called social justice warriors and their left-wing allies today, nor would he conduct himself in the same manner as groups like Black Lives Matter. King valued personal responsibility, not welfare dependence; believed individuals should be judged by the content of their character, not race and identity politics; and thought social movements should make use of peaceful protest, not violence and rioting.

Out of all the insane claims the right makes, this is right up there at the top of the list. During the last years of King's life, the likes of Barry Goldwater and his supporters were taking over the Republican Party. Goldwater gained support by pandering to racist southern whites, opposing the 1964 Civil Rights Act. King saw exactly what the Republican Party was turning into. That's why he urged Americans to vote against Goldwater and criticized the Republican Party for its "racism, reaction, and extremism."[71] King even claimed that the Republican Party would lead America down a "fascist path."[72] In 1968 King also criticized the Party for promoting Ronald Reagan as a potential presidential candidate, characterizing Reagan as a "Hollywood performer, lacking distinction." King also derided Reagan as a "war hawk."[73] If King would have lived, he would have seen Richard Nixon drag his feet when enforcing school integration, pander to segregationists by attempting to appoint southerners to the Supreme Court, and exploit racial unrest in America's cities, where protests erupted in response to racist housing policies and police brutality.[74] King would have also seen the Republican Party oppose making King's own birthday a national holiday based on the claim that the holiday would cost too much money, even as Republicans were exploding the deficit with arms build-ups, illegal wars, and tax cuts for the rich.[75]

King's economic views were also antithetical to the Republican Party's. "I am much more socialistic in my economic theory than capitalistic," King wrote in a letter to his future wife.[76] King believed that "capitalism has outlived its usefulness" and, in a 1961 speech to the Negro American Labor Council, stated, "Call it democracy, or call it democratic socialism, but there must be a better distribution of wealth within this country for all God's children."[77] Not exactly the main plank of the Republican Party. King's pronouncements weren't just words. When King was assassinated, he was in Memphis to support striking sanitation workers who demanded higher wages and better working conditions.

There's no reason to believe King's views would have changed. Conservative majorities on the Supreme Court halted school integration by overturning busing laws and fueled economic inequality by denying equal funding for public schools.[78] The right has also spent decades busting unions, slashing social programs, cutting taxes for the rich, using monetary policy to depress wages, letting the minimum wage erode, entering into trade agreements that allow corporations to offshore jobs, and slashing public sector jobs (disproportionately held by blacks). All of these policies converge to weaken the bargaining power of the working class and ensure persistently high levels of poverty and economic insecurity.[79] In order to prevent the poor from changing this system, the Republican Party adopted the same strategy once used by southern Democrats to disenfranchise black voters. Whereas Democrats in the Jim Crow South used poll taxes, literacy tests, and violence to keep blacks from voting, Republicans pass voter ID laws, restrict voting hours, limit early voting, reduce the number of voting machines in Democratic precincts, eliminate same-day voter registration, purge voter rolls, engage in voter caging, empower state officials to challenge mail-in ballots, and support felon disenfranchisement laws.[80]

When groups like Black Lives Matter protest these social and economic injustices, along with many other racist practices, for example racial profiling, police brutality, racial disparities in conviction rates and criminal sentencing, and so on, King would have seen the right brand these protesters as violent "thugs" in order to discredit them, just as segregationists did to King decades ago. It's silly to think King would support a political movement that would use these tactics today. Black Lives Matter and the recent protests we've seen around the country carry the same moral legitimacy as the protests King led, especially given the glacial pace of change on matters of economic justice since King's day. No doubt King would be marching side-by-side with these protesters, not supporting the people trying to crush them while cynically attempting to co-opt King's legacy.

This isn't to say that King would fully support the modern Democratic Party. During the final years of King's life, much of the Democratic Party establishment despised King, and since King's death, Democrats have largely stood by—and indeed have been complicit in—implementing much of the right's agenda. But to claim that King would be a conservative today, let alone a Republican, is laughable. The right's attempt to claim Martin Luther King as one of their own is an insult to King's legacy—a dishonest attempt to mask the perverse nature of the Republican Party's economic agenda, which is meant to enrich the few, and has devastating effects for the poor.

CHAPTER EIGHT

The PC Thought Police

According to the right, liberals and the left are imposing a totalitarian form of thought control on the rest of society. Most of the mainstream media has a liberal bias and controls the flow of information throughout society to promote "fake news" and brainwash the public into accepting liberal political and economic views. To support this claim, the right points to the fact that most journalists vote Democrat, as well as the fact that newspapers like *The New York Times* always endorse Democratic political candidates. The right also cites media coverage of Donald Trump's presidency, which was overwhelmingly negative, in order to bolster their claim that the media is biased. Liberals and the left also stifle free speech by shaming the rest of society into using politically correct terminology, shouting down right-wing speakers on college campuses, and partnering with tech companies like Facebook and Google to censor right-wing views on the Internet. Each of these tactics supposedly limits how we think and talk about important issues.

Fueling this problem is a phenomena the right denigrates as "identity politics." According to the right, those who ascribe to various group identities, whether members of the LGBTQ community, African Americans, women, Marxists, Democrats, and so on, aim to tear down American society and use their control over culture, politics, and the media to distort the truth, substituting "victim narratives" in its place. So-called victims use these tactics to gain sympathy, "take power," then silence anyone who disagrees with them.

It's hard to listen to these hysterics and keep a straight face. The media is owned by giant corporate conglomerates whose aim is to make a profit. They make profits by selling advertisements to affluent consumers and receiving massive subsidies from the political, business, and military establishment. This ensures that whatever liberal bias is reflected in the media skews from center-right to right—especially on economic issues and foreign policy. While the media often disagrees with the right on many social issues, such as abortion, gun control, and gay rights, we'll see that this isn't true when it comes to issues having to do with the fundamental nature of the American economy or the distribution of wealth and power that arises within the economy.

It's understandable why the right has been able to spread the myth that the media has a liberal or left-wing bias. Cultural and social issues tend to dominate the headlines, on which the liberal and right-wing establishment often disagree; and because slight differences in opinion on economic issues, for example whether or not we should expand domestic oil production to alleviate high gas prices, or whether or not to adopt moderate reforms such as Obamacare to fix America's broken healthcare system (as opposed to nationalizing the oil industry to control prices or establishing a single-payer healthcare system), are presented as representing two extremes, defined as "the left" and "the right." It's also true that identity politics plays a role in the media's coverage of the issues. Liberal elites have co-opted identity politics for their own benefit. When the media champions issues that are important to various group identities, for example LGBTQ rights or opposition to police brutality, or gun control, media figures can pat themselves on the back because they view themselves as taking a stand in support of social justice. This provides the right with evidence to support the claim that the media has a liberal bias. The right then conflates elite liberal opinion with "the left," while branding identity politics itself as left-wing, even though this is far from the truth.

Even worse, this "two sides" framework assumes that each "side" should be given equal attention regardless of the merit of either side's position. This skews media coverage to the right. If the right pushes climate change denial, for example, according to the right these views should be given equal air time to warnings about the dangers of climate change, even though climate change denial has no scientific basis. Right-wing views are therefore *overrepresented* in the media—the opposite of what the right claims.

Nor does the right value free speech. If efforts to get others to use politically correct terminology limits speech, then the right is just as guilty of violating free speech as anyone. They have their own politically correct terminology, which they use to erode empathy for vulnerable groups, and therefore erode support for policies meant to help these groups, for example social welfare programs.

The right also exaggerates the threat to free speech posed by political correctness and cancel culture. Campus protests aimed at right-wing speakers, for example, are relatively rare, and have little effect on the ability of these speakers to spread their ideas. The right also has no problem when employers fire their employees for their political views, when the police jail protesters, or when the FBI places disempowered communities under surveillance, and so on.

The same is true regarding censorship at the hands of major tech companies. While the right complains when Facebook, Amazon, and Google, censor their users, the right also does everything they can to empower these companies by slashing regulations and corporate tax rates. These policies fuel economic inequality, and concentrate power into the hands of tech companies, along with other media conglomerates, who use their power to spread pro-business propaganda and drown out the speech of those with fewer resources, limiting their ability to have their speech heard. Indeed, the right misses the entire point of free speech, which is to affect social change. But the form of social change the left advocates is nearly impossible given the extreme level of economic inequality that pervades American society, for which the right is primarily responsible.

Nor does the right have any problem with "identity politics." The right views itself as the embodiment of America's "true" identity—white, Christian, law-abiding, "taxpayers" who just want the government to leave them alone. Also recall the right's claim that the goal of identity politics is to "take power." This is no less true of the right's brand of identity politics, only there's no need for the right to take power, since those who share their identity are the ones who've traditionally wielded the most power in American society, and still do. However, they'll do anything they can to maintain this power—for example, by erecting political barriers against democracy, or by spreading propaganda meant to erode empathy for the disadvantaged, instead portraying themselves as victims.

The right's form of identity politics, far from promoting the truth, aims to create an alternate reality. Thus climate change is a liberal hoax, Democrats stole the 2020 election, and Hillary Clinton is a pedophile who literally eats children. These insane beliefs are fueled by cable news and social media, which create echo chambers that amplify the right's propaganda, and whip those who consume this propaganda into a perpetual state of anger and resentment towards out-groups who lack actual power in society. Fake issues, like transgender bathrooms, a toy company re-branding Mr. Potatohead, or what actors and athletes have to say about various issues, come to dominate every day conversation, distracting from real issues that actually affect peoples' lives. In the meantime, institutions that perpetuate injustice remain unchanged, much to the delight of the elites who benefit from these institutions.

The Liberal Media

The right claims the media has a liberal bias. They point out that most journalists are registered Democrats. Many donate to Democratic politicians. Newspapers such as *The New York Times* and *The Washington Post* always endorse Democratic presidential candidates. The media's coverage of Donald Trump was overwhelmingly negative. According to the right, these facts show that liberals have greater control over the flow of information throughout society, allowing them to brainwash the public into accepting their political and cultural agenda, while marginalizing the right's ideas. The right, however, has no clue how the media actually works.

The media is biased towards the political, military, and business establishment. These overlapping centers of American power supply the media with an army of "experts" to provide content—politicians who love to be in front of the camera, ex-military who serve on the boards of major defense contractors, flunkies who work for pro-business think tanks, etc. This provides the media with an enormous subsidy. The media relies on these figures to fill up airtime, lend themselves credibility, and limit costs. Prominent media figures often run in the same social circles as these experts and belong to the same "beltway" culture. They attend the same banquets. Their kids attend the same private schools. And so on. The media therefore has a number of incentives not to challenge their guests too hard on controversial issues. Instead, they offer them a great deal of deference, allowing them to spread propaganda.[1]

But the political, military, and business establishment are hardly "liberal." While liberals do make up half of the establishment, so do business figures who hold right-wing political and economic views, Republican politicians who represent these interests, and hawkish military figures who not only believe the US military is a force for good in the world, but stand to gain financially from more aggressive US foreign policy. The liberals who comprise part of this establishment also tend to either be economic elites, or represent elite interests. While many of them hold progressive views when it comes to issues like race and gender, gun control, and abortion, the same can hardly be said for their economic views. When Nancy Pelosi goes on CNN to smugly proclaim "we're capitalist" in response to an audience member pointing out that a majority of young adults no longer support capitalism, or when Joe Manchin pens an op-ed voicing opposition to expanded voting rights, these figures are espousing positions to the right of a large segment of their liberal constituents.[2]

Also note that while the establishment includes liberal elites, this isn't what the right means by "liberal." The right conflates the liberal establishment with the left, and thus uses the terms "liberal media" and "left-wing media" interchangeably, even though the liberal establishment and the left have far different political agendas. It's misleading to claim that the media has a left-wing bias if what the right means by left-wing are figures like Hillary Clinton and Nancy Pelosi. Media bias therefore tends to skew from center-left to right on social justice issues—which have little effect on the economic power of the corporate elite—and center-right to right on economic issues and foreign policy. If you want to call this "liberal," fine. But all this means is that "liberal" reflects a spectrum of opinion that skews to the right, not a spectrum that includes left-wing views.

In order to see how the establishment enjoys so much influence over the media, it's also important to understand that the media is owned by giant corporate conglomerates whose aim is to make a profit. They do this by selling audiences to advertisers, not by doing good journalism, or catering to left-wing audiences.[3] These advertisers want to reach affluent consumers who can afford to buy their spouse a Lexus SUV for Christmas or TD Ameritrade "investment" products. This audience tends to skew from center-left to far right. Advertisers also understand that left-wing policies are a threat to their bottom line. While an advertiser might boycott a Fox News host if the host says something perceived as racist, because the advertiser doesn't want their brand associated with racist views, the possibility of losing sales by pulling ads from Fox News doesn't threaten the power of advertisers in the same way that promoting a higher corporate tax rate, universal public healthcare, or stronger unions would. It's unlikely that corporations would spend money advertising on shows that promote these policies.

Nor does the fact that journalists tend to be registered Democrats show the media has a liberal bias. Media personalities hardly share the views of ordinary Democratic voters—especially when it comes to US foreign policy—and most don't hold left-wing economic views. Journalists who hold left-wing views are all but precluded from gaining prominent positions in the mainstream media. It's not like these figures hire themselves. Those who make hiring decisions in the media aren't leftists, but elites that sit on the boards of media companies,[4] and corporate executives whose job is to boost ad revenue by catering to affluent audiences that—again—fall somewhere between center-left and the far right along the political spectrum. Journalists likely to gain prominent positions in the media also tend to come from privileged backgrounds, attend elite universities, are likely to have internalized establishment positions and accept the existing economic order as a given rather than question this order, and are unlikely to support drastic levels of wealth redistribution that would threaten their own material interests.

But this is almost beside the point. If the media is supposed to present ideas based on whether these ideas actually hold water, then the right's over-representation in the media is even more pronounced. The right has spent decades pouring billions of dollars into magazines, think tanks, radio programming, websites, and advertising to spread their ideas, as well as discipline rival outlets who fail to promote these ideas *even though these ideas are intellectually bankrupt*. This is often done in the name of ensuring "balance." But what's meant by balance has nothing to do with balance in any normal sense—for example, balance when presenting evidence in support of one position or another, or balance when presenting a range of viewpoints of interest to the public. It means balance of opinion between different wings of the establishment. From the right's perspective, what matters is whether the media *promotes the right's views*. It doesn't matter, for example, if there's no empirical evidence that tax cuts for the rich do anything other than benefit the rich, or that climate change is a liberal hoax. Yet if the right's views aren't adequately reflected in the media, the right brands the media as "socialists" and purveyors of media bias—and does so incessantly.[5] While the right would probably do this no matter what, the fact that the media isn't accountable to the left makes it more likely that right-wing flak will succeed in preventing the media from giving left-wing ideas more prominence—like redistributive economic policies or a Green New Deal—and give the right's ideas outsized influence relative to their actual merit.

The reason many are so easily tricked into believing the media has a "liberal" or "left-wing" bias is because within the narrow range of views reflected in the media, the media presents opposing viewpoints as representing two extremes.[6] The best example of this is the media's coverage of Donald Trump. Liberals in the media obsessed over Trump's uncouth behavior, branding him as a liar, a racist, a "populist," and so on. This self-serving narrative allowed the media to brand itself as doing "tough," antagonistic journalism, acting as part of "The Resistance" in order to hold executive authority accountable. The media, however, paid almost no attention to the reasons Trump was able to gain power in the first place—which in no small part was due to voters being fed up with the corruption of Democratic Party elites. Meanwhile, the right attacked the media as being snobbish elites, while laughing all the way to the bank by passing massive tax cuts for the rich.

Liberal bias in the media—insofar as "liberal" refers to ordinary liberal voters or the left—is a myth. The right only wants to make it seem as if the media is much further to the left than it is in reality, so the right can mobilize its base, win elections, and implement an economic agenda that serves the interests of the most powerful sectors of American society.

Free Speech

According to the right, our freedom of speech is under threat. Liberals and the left are over-sensitive "snowflakes" who get "triggered" when they hear something offensive. In response, they try to force the rest of society to use "politically correct" terminology. If others don't adopt this terminology, they're accused of being racists, homophobes, and misogynists. This drama plays out most vividly on college campuses, where the left apparently enjoys total control of the culture. In this environment, left-wing protesters shout down right-wing speakers, supposedly violating the right's freedom of speech. These tactics also extend to social media, whereby anyone espousing politically incorrect views is "canceled" by technology companies, such as Facebook, Google, and Amazon. According to the right, these anti-free speech tactics amount to a totalitarian form of thought control. The right, however, doesn't actually care about free speech.

The right is the biggest bunch of PC crybabies to ever exist. To see why, just point out these obviously true things: that American settlers committed genocide against Native Americans, that capitalism was initially fueled by slave labor, that the US tortures Muslims, that right-wing Christians commit more terrorism in the US than Muslims, that the US has been responsible for the bulk of violence around the world since the end of World War II, or—God forbid—that rich people don't earn their wealth or deserve to keep it. You'll never see a bigger bunch of snowflakes get triggered more quickly. Instead of admitting these truths, the right uses their own politically correct terminology. Native Americans just "died of disease." We don't torture Muslims; we use "enhanced interrogation techniques." White nationalists aren't terrorists, but "mentally unstable individuals." The rich aren't leeching on society; they "earn" their wealth through "hard work," "sacrifice," and "risk." Donald Trump isn't a racist; he's just "telling it like it is." Police don't murder unarmed suspects, but are "involved in shootings." Right-wing death squads in Central America aren't terrorists, but "freedom fighters." You get the picture.

It's understandable why the right would want to portray the left's use of PC terminology as harmful, while ignoring how the right uses their own PC terminology. The left's terminology is meant to expose injustice, empathize with others, and bolster democracy. Marginalized groups face legitimate problems, such as discrimination, enormous disparities in income and wealth, and in some cases surveillance, or even murder. Liberals and the left use language they believe is sensitive to these injustices. This poses a threat to the right's corporate backers. If more people sympathize with those who suffer injustice, and as a result decide to use the political system to do something about it, the system under which elites on the right benefit might come under threat. The right's PC terminology is therefore meant to conceal injustice, undermine empathy for the disadvantaged, and destroy democracy, with the aim of protecting society's most privileged members.

We also know the right doesn't care about free speech by looking at the actions of their political leaders. Right-wing lawmakers in a number of states have recently attempted to introduce legislation that makes it illegal to boycott Israel, allows law enforcement to deem any assembly illegal, criminalizes protests that block traffic, prohibits public employees from striking, punishes those who protest oil and gas pipelines, expels children for not standing for the Pledge of Allegiance, deports legal immigrants who engage in protest, defines protests as "riots," recategorizes minor offenses for protesting as felonies, denies protesters bail, bans teachings about slavery in schools, and so on.[7] These are far more serious threats to free speech than political correctness. Yet the right gladly supports these forms of repression.

This is how it's always been. During the late nineteenth and early twentieth centuries, states made it illegal to belong to labor organizations such as the IWW, corporations used private goon squads, as well as police and the military, to beat up workers who attempted to organize; as well as relied on the government to toss socialist leaders in jail for their political views. During the 1950s, the right branded anyone who held even moderately left-wing views as a "communist," often ruining their reputations and costing them their careers and therefore their livelihoods.[8] The right's recent efforts to silence their opponents are just the latest in a long history of political repression that makes current efforts by liberals and the left look like a joke.

Indeed, the right wildly exaggerates the supposed threat campus protests pose to free speech. There were only 36 disruptions across 4,700 university campuses in 2017.[9] The supposed campus speech crisis is a public relations campaign funded by billionaires like the Kochs and the DeVos family to gain control of universities. These groups spend millions of dollars funding departments and centers like the Mercatus Center at George Mason University and the James Madison Center for Free Speech, which promote ideas that legitimize corporate control of the economic system.[10] The right wants to create a safe space for their ideas, even though these ideas have no more intellectual merit than the ideas promoted by the Flat Earth Society.

If we want to understand the threat posed by campus protests, we might also examine the actual effect of these protests. What typically happens in these cases is that the speakers who get "shut down" by protests just move on to more speaking gigs, then go back to their TV shows and claim to millions of viewers that the right is being "canceled," drumming up fake outrage among their base of followers while right-wing politicians use their outsized political power to enact the types of repression listed above. Campus protests therefore have the opposite of their intended effect. It's hard to take the right seriously when they exaggerate the scale and effect of these protests, while supporting far more serious forms of repression.

But there are other reasons we know the right doesn't care about free speech on college campuses. When professors express views the right doesn't agree with, right-wing groups harass and intimidate these professors, or launch smear campaigns against them. These tactics have caused professors to be denied tenure, fired, or harassed into silence. This is especially true when it comes to the Israel-Palestine conflict. When pro-Israel groups like StandWithUs and Canary Mission employ these tactics against those who speak out against Israel's harsh policies, the right remains silent. The right only cries foul when speakers funded by right-wing think tanks and Koch money are shouted down.[11]

The same is true of employment more generally. The most pernicious forms of cancel culture occur in the workplace. Employers limit the speech of their employees under the threat (real or implied) of termination. This can have a devastating impact on ordinary people's lives. When figures like Ben Shapiro have a lecture canceled on a college campus, they can go back onto their media platforms, continue to reach millions of listeners, and rake in millions of dollars. But ordinary people can be deprived of their entire livelihoods for expressing political views their employer doesn't like. Indeed, there is no shortage of snitches on the right who will tattle on you to your boss and try to get you fired for saying something offensive on social media.[12]

But what about Google, Facebook, and Amazon? Don't these companies censor right-wing views, and isn't this a problem? Of course. But the problem with these companies is that we cede too much power to corporations in general. If the right valued free speech, they wouldn't seek to lower these companies' taxes or refuse to break up these companies. It's only the left that wants to do this. Better yet, we could nationalize these companies, so the First Amendment would apply to speech on their platforms. This type of government action, however, threatens the interests of the right far more than getting "de-platformed." It's the wealth the rich accumulate from investing in large corporations that gives the right far greater influence in society than being able to post on Twitter.

What these examples show is that debates about "free speech" in the US are incoherent. The point of free speech is to affect social change. But our ability to use speech in this way is undermined to the point of irrelevance by America's highly skewed distribution of wealth. In the US, everyone in theory has the same right to speak, yet those with more wealth have far greater ability to both have their ideas heard and to affect change in society.[13] The right in particular has outsized power in this regard. Corporations have spent billions of dollars funding think tanks and lobbying groups to spread the right's ideas, astroturf political movements, corrupt politicians, and write laws that generate greater levels of economic inequality. If the right really cared about free speech, they would do the opposite. But it's not in their interest to do so.

The right doesn't care about free speech. They exploit the fact that we value free speech in order to further their own economic and political agenda. They promote their own version of political correctness to erode empathy for the economically disadvantaged, employ political repression to silence their enemies on the left, and have no problem with cancel culture when it comes to bosses canceling their employees. As long as it allows the rich to maintain their wealth and privilege, when it comes to violating free speech the right doesn't even bat an eye.

Identity Politics

The right constantly rails against "identity politics." They claim that those who identify as members of various groups—LGBTQ, black, women, Marxists, etc.—along with their allies in the government, academia, and the media, aim to "tear down" American society and culture. These groups reject history in favor of "victim narratives," according to the right, and therefore reject objective truth, making it impossible to engage in reasoned discourse. These groups supposedly see culture and politics as a means by which to "take power" and impose their views on the rest of society. According to the right, these tactics are an attack on "freedom," whereby those who don't conform to the views of "social justice warriors" are "silenced." The right's proclamations about identity politics, however, paint a wildly distorted picture of what those who've embraced identity politics generally believe.

Identity politics isn't about tearing down American culture, embracing "victim narratives," rejecting truth or morality, "taking power," or forcing one's views on the rest of society. Rather, those who've embraced identity politics aim to bring about a pluralistic, multicultural society that acknowledges perspectives that have traditionally been marginalized. Far from rejecting history in favor of victim narratives, they aim to shed light on the actual history of oppression—which is too often omitted from standard versions of history we were taught in school. Far from "taking power," it's more accurate to claim that those who associate with various identities wish to claim their own *share* of power—which they've historically lacked. Rather than forcing their views on the rest of society, they believe those in power should be called out when they refuse to acknowledge alternate perspectives, because when they don't, society will never learn the lessons of the past, those who face disadvantages will remain in this position, and history will be doomed to repeat itself. Whether or not this strategy is effective or wise, the point is to foster empathy for others, particularly those who consider themselves among groups that have historically faced oppression, the residual effects of which continue to harm millions of people.

None of this is to say we should embrace identity politics. Indeed, much of the left views identity politics in a negative light, since it diminishes the role class plays in society, and splinters what might otherwise form a powerful coalition rooted in common economic interests into disarray.[14] The left views those who embrace identity politics as having given up hope that any viable alternative to capitalism might emerge to re-order society on a more egalitarian basis, so they might as well get on board and settle for more women CEOs and high-ranking political officials. This is a shame. Economic elites would love nothing more than for their opposition to remain divided and their power to act as a counterweight to capital dispersed.

Even more problematic, however, is that the right has fully embraced identity politics, only on steroids. Everything the right points out is wrong with identity politics has come to characterize the right itself—but in the worst possible way. Rather than aiming to bring about a pluralistic, multicultural society that embraces a wide variety of perspectives, the right aims to preserve America's "true" identity—white, Christian, "patriots" who just "love freedom"—while continuing to marginalize perspectives that differ from their own. Rather than associating with identities that have suffered oppression at the hands of the powerful, the right identifies with those who've traditionally wielded the most power in society. Rather than aiming to secure some share of power for one's identity through democratic politics, the right aims to maintain their control over the political system using undemocratic means. Rather than promoting different viewpoints to foster empathy for those who face injustice, the right promotes views that erode empathy for those who face injustice—then rejects views that run contrary to the right's interests as "fake news."[15]

And it's only getting worse. The right's deranged form of identity politics is fueled by cable news and social media, which constantly bombard us with information from an endless number of sources, who compete with each other and must therefore engage in oneupmanship to gain our attention. These outlets use soundbites, sensationalist headlines, summaries, and memes, which are devoid of substance. This turns politics into a form of entertainment, where every story must be given a hyperbolic, partisan spin, or attempt to "trigger" or "own" the "other side." These mediums erode our capacity to engage in serious analysis, fuel political partisanship, mobilize anxieties, amplify feelings of victimization, stoke resentment, and direct aggression against one's perceived enemies.[16]

These developments have had a corrosive effect on American political discourse, and therefore democracy. Social media has largely replaced in-person, one-to-one interaction, placing individuals outside of their communities and into fake, inauthentic, online "communities" with others who have like-minded views, isolating them from contact with those who have different perspectives. Individuals can pick what they want to believe and find any number of justifications to support these beliefs—including baseless conspiracy theories—while having those beliefs reinforced by others who inhabit the same echo chamber, rehearse right-wing talking points, and egg each other on. In the process, the right has lost its ability to distinguish between image and reality.[17]

Liberals are hardly immune from these phenomena. They latch on to their own social and political authorities, swallow conspiracies from media outlets like MSNBC and CNN, and are quick to dismiss the right as racist hillbillies rather than come to terms with the failings of their own political leaders and information sources—which have bred widespread resentment and cynicism that elites have exploited for authoritarian ends. These include figures like Donald Trump, who used populist rhetoric to get elected, only to support a reactionary agenda once in power; the liberal politicians who supported slimy institutions, such as the FBI, in order to attack Trump; or those who supported the merger of government and Big Tech to censor the views of their political opposition on both the right and the left.

The right, however, is on another plane. They dismiss any information that contradicts their beliefs, instead looking to "intellectuals" like Dinesh D'Souza and Ben Shapiro, "investigative journalists" like James O'Keefe and Andy Ngo, and fake YouTube "universities" like Prager U. These hucksters serve no one but the Republican Party and much of the corporate elite, without even the pretense of integrity or journalistic standards. While it would be an understatement to say there are serious problems with the mainstream media, the right has come to trust sources that are less reliable and have even less integrity, while fully embracing the military, business, and Republican Party establishment, along with fascist goon squads like ICE and police who murder defenseless citizens. The right uses identity politics as an excuse to think and do whatever they want, becoming a crude caricature of what they claim to despise. So yes, identity politics is a problem. But if the right is serious in its opposition to identity politics, they need to look in the mirror.

Notes

CHAPTER ONE: CONSERVATISM

1. Mark Levin, *Liberty and Tyranny: A Conservative Manifesto* (New York: Threshold Editions, 2009), 14.
2. Peter Linebaugh, *The Magna Carta Manifesto: Liberties and Commons for All* (Berkeley: University of California Press, 2008).
3. Jason Hickel, *The Divide: Global Inequality from Conquest to Free Markets* (New York: W. W. Norton & Company, 2018), 73-79.
4. Thomas Jefferson, letter to James Madison, 1785.
5. Ibid.
6. Keri Leigh Merrit, *Masterless Men: Poor Whites and Slavery in the Antebellum South* (Cambridge: Cambridge University Press, 2017).
7. Steven Stoll, *Ramp Hollow: The Ordeal of Appalachia* (United States: Farrar, Straus and Giroux, 2017).
8. Ibid., 176-211.
9. Elizabeth Anderson, *Private Government: How Employers Rule Our Lives (and Why We Don't Talk About It)* (Princeton: Princeton University Press, 2017), 33-36.
10. Ibid., 32-33.

11 Eric Foner, *Reconstruction: America's Unfinished Revolution, 1863-1877* (New York: Harper Collins, 1989), 166-167.
12 Thomas Sugrue, *The Origins of the Urban Crisis: Race and Inequality in Postwar Detroit* (Princeton: Princeton University Press, 1996), 91-124.
13 Ibid., 125-130; Jefferson Cowie, *Capital Moves: RCA's Seventy-Year Quest for Cheap Labor* (New York: The New Press, 2001), 41-126.
14 On the drivers of economic inequality in recent decades, see: Dean Baker, *The Conservative Nanny State: How the Rich Use the Government to Stay Rich and Get Richer* (Washington, DC: Center for Economic and Policy Research, 2006); Dean Baker, *Rigged: How Globalization and the Rules of the Modern Economy Were Structured to Make the Rich Richer* (Washington, D.C.: Center for Economic and Policy Research, 2016); Adam Cohen, *Supreme Inequality: The Supreme Court's Fifty-Year Battle for a More Unjust America* (United States: Penguin Press, 2020); Cowie, *Capital Moves*; Christopher Faricy, *Welfare for the Wealthy: Parties, Social Spending, and Inequality in the United States* (Cambridge: Cambridge University Press, 2016); Jacob Hacker and Paul Pierson, *Winner-Take-All Politics: How Washington Made the Rich Richer—And Turned Its Back on the Middle Class* (New York: Simon & Shuster, 2010); Gordon Lafer, *The One Percent Solution: How Corporations Are Remaking America One State at a Time* (Ithaca: ILR Press, 2017).
15 Anu Partanen, *The Nordic Theory of Everything: In Search of a Better Life* (New York: Harper, 2016), 96-102.
16 Aviva Chomsky, *Undocumented: How Immigration Became Illegal* (Boston: Beacon Press, 2014), 117-151.
17 Edward Baptist, *The Half Has Never Been Told: Slavery and the Making of American Capitalism* (New York: Basic Books, 2014).
18 John Tirman, *The Deaths of Others: The Fate of Civilians in America's Wars* (New York: Oxford University Press, 2011), 92, 168.
19 Vincent Bevins, *The Jakarta Method: Washington's Anticommunist Crusade & The Mass Murder Program That Shaped Our Wold* (New York: Hatchette Book Group, Inc., 2020).
20 Hickel, *The Divide*, 113, 197.
21 Charles Sellers, *The Market Revolution: Jacksonian America, 1815-1846* (New York: Oxford University Press, 1991), 1-201.
22 Norman Ware, *The Industrial Worker, 1840-1860: The Reaction of American Industrial Society to the Advance of the Industrial Revolution* (New York: Houghton Mifflin, 1924), 6-9, 26-100.
23 Sellers, *The Market Revolution*, 341.
24 Anderson, *Private Government*, 33-36.
25 William Blizzard, *When Miners March* (Oakland: PM Press, 2010), 341.
26 Michael Yates, *Why Unions Matter* (New York: Monthly Review Press, 2009), 50,

188-189.
27 Karl Polanyi, *The Great Transformation: The Political and Economic Origins of Our Time* (Boston: Beacon Press, 2001).
28 See note 14.
29 Noam Chomsky and Robert Polin, *Climate Crisis and the Global Green New Deal: The Political Economy of Saving the Planet* (New York: Verso, 2020).
30 Katharina Pistor, *The Code of Capital: How the Law Creates Wealth and Inequality* (Princeton: Princeton University Press, 2019), 34.
31 Morton Horwitz, *The Transformation of American Law, 1780-1860* (Cambridge: Harvard University Press, 1977), 40-41.
32 Thomas Jefferson, letter to James Madison, 1785.
33 Benjamin Franklin, letter to Robert Morris, 1783.
34 Thomas Paine, *Agrarian Justice*, 1797.
35 David Korten, *When Corporations Rule the World* (San Francisco: Berrett-Koehler Publishers, 2001), 63.
36 Horwitz, *The Transformation of American Law*, 46-47.
37 Horwitz, *The Transformation of American Law*.
38 Karen Orren, *Belated Feudalism: Labor, the Law, and Liberal Development in the United States* (New York: Cambridge University Press, 1991), 89-91.
39 Ibid., 93.
40 Ibid., 122, 129, 133; Ted Nace, *Gangs of America: The Rise of Corporate Power and the Disabling of Democracy* (San Francisco: Berret-Koehler Publishers, Inc., 2005), 125.
41 Anderson, *Private Government*, 33-36.
42 Christopher Tiedeman, *A Treatise on State and Federal Control of Persons and Property in the United States Considered from Both a Civil and Criminal Standpoint* (Union: The Lawbook Exchange, 2002), 383, 609-610.
43 Naomi Lamoreaux and William Novak, eds., *Corporations and American Democracy* (Cambridge: Harvard University Press, 2017), 114, Kindle.
44 Robert Post, *Citizens Divided: Campaign Finance Reform and the Constitution* (Cambridge: Harvard University Press, 2014), 29.
45 Nace, *Gangs of America*, 244-248.
46 Ibid., 127-129.
47 Lamoreaux and Novak, *Corporations and American Democracy*, 115.
48 Cohen. *Supreme Inequality*, 314-315.
49 Ibid., 1-40.
50 Cohen, *Supreme Inequality*.
51 Mark Levin, "The Modern Democrats' Rejection Of Private Property Rights," YouTube, August 1, 2012, 9:01, https://www.youtube.com/watch?v=aCqRkQzYkiU.

52 Matt Bruenig, "Top 1% Up $21 Trillion. Bottom 50% Down $900 Billion," *People's Policy Project*, Jun. 14, 2019, https://www.peoplespolicyproject.org/2019/06/14/top-1-up-21-trillion-bottom-50-down-900-billion/.
53 See note 14.
54 Mark Levin, *Ameritopia: The Unmaking of America* (New York: Threshold Editions, 2012), 9.
55 Thomas Piketty, *Capital in the Twenty-First Century* (Cambridge: The Bellknap Press, 2014), 512.
56 Rob Larson, *Bit Tyrants: The Political Economy of Silicon Valley* (Chicago: Haymarket Books, 2020), 29-35.
57 Robert Jackall, *Moral Mazes: The World of Corporate Managers* (Oxford: Oxford University Press, 2010), 18-94.
58 Lane Kenworthy, *Social Democratic America* (New York: Oxford University Press, 2014), 33-34.

CHAPTER TWO: CLASSICAL LIBERALISM

1 Anderson, *Private Government*, 4.
2 Matt Bruenig, "Top 1% Up $21 Trillion. Bottom 50% Down $900 Billion," *People's Policy Project*, June 14, 2019, https://www.peoplespolicyproject.org/2019/06/14/top-1-up-21-trillion-bottom-50-down-900-billion/.
3 Adam Smith, *The Wealth of Nations* (New York: Bantam Dell, 2003), 1084-1085.
4 Robert Nozick, *Anarchy, State, and Utopia* (Malden: Blackwell Publishing, 2009), 174-175.
5 John Locke, *Second Treatise of Government* (Mineola: Dover Publications, Inc., 2002), 15-16; Will Kymlicka, *Contemporary Political Philosophy: An Introduction* (New York: Oxford University Press, 1990), 108-112.
6 John Locke, *First Treatise of Government*, para. 42.
7 C.B Macpherson, *The Political Theory of Possessive Individualism: Hobbes to Locke* (Oxford: Oxford University Press, 2011), 5.
8 Gar Alperowitz and Lew Daly, *Unjust Deserts: How the Rich Are Taking Our Common Inheritance and Why We Should Take It Back* (New York: The New Press, 2008), 25-26.
9 Matt Bruenig, "Massive Rise of Top Incomes Is Mostly Driven By Capital," *People's Policy Project*, Aug. 9, 2017, https://www.peoplespolicyproject.org/2017/08/09/massive-rise-of-top-incomes-is-mostly-driven-by-capital/.
10 Alperowitz and Daly, *Unjust Deserts*, 98-177.
11 Schweickart, *Against Capitalism*, 29-42.
12 Kymlicka, *Contemporary Political Philosophy*, 114.

13　Foner, *Reconstruction*, 166-167.
14　William Blizzard, *When Miners March* (Oakland: PM Press, 2010), 26-27, 35, 48-49, 101-106.
15　Chomsky, *Undocumented*, 117-151.
16　Anderson, *Private Government*, 4.
17　Ken Klippenstein, "Documents Show Amazon Aware Drivers Pee in Bottles and Even Defecate En Route, Despite Company Denial," *The Intercept*, March 25, 2021, https://theintercept.com/2021/03/25/amazon-drivers-pee-bottles-union/.
18　Smith, *The Wealth of Nations*, 23-24.
19　Anderson, *Private Government*, 21.
20　Ibid., 33-36.
21　Smith, *The Wealth of Nations*, 987.
22　Ibid., 177.
23　Tiedeman, *A Treatise on State and Federal Control of Persons and Property in the United States Considered from Both a Civil and Criminal Standpoint* (St. Louis: The F.H. Thomas Law Book Co., 1900) 383, 609-610.

CHAPTER THREE: CONSTITUTIONALISM

1　Richard Morris, *The Forging of the Union 1781–1789* (New York: Harper & Row, 1987), 31-54, 148-152, 158-159.
2　Michael Klarman, *The Framers' Coup: The Making of the United States Constitution* (New York: Oxford University Press, 2016), 130, 133.
3　Ibid., 371-372.
4　Jennifer Nedelsky, *Private Property and the Limits of American Constitutionalism: The Madisonian Framework and Its Legacy* (Chicago: University of Chicago Press, 1990), 23-23.
5　Noam Chomsky, *Profit Over People: Neoliberalism and Global Order* (New York: Seven Stories Press, 1999), 46.
6　Klarman, *The Framers' Coup*, 210.
7　Chomsky, *Profit Over People*, 51-52.
8　Klarman, *The Framers' Coup*, 178-179.
9　Alexis de Tocqueville, *Democracy in America* (United States: Penguin Putnam Inc., 2004), 648.
10　Blizzard, *When Miners March*, 26-27, 35, 48-49, 101-106; Anderson, *Private Government*, 33-36.
11　Chomsky, *Undocumented*, 117-151.
12　Pauline Maier, *Ratification: The People Debate the Constitution, 1787-1788* (New York: Simon & Shuster, 2011), 84-85.

13 James Madison, "The Meaning of the Constitution," (Address to Congress, April 6, 1796).
14 Klarman, *The Framers' Coup*, 298.
15 Ibid., 310.
16 Ibid., 358.
17 Maier, *Ratification*, 203-204.
18 Ibid., 67-68.
19 Klarman, *The Framers' Coup*, 509; Maier, *Ratification*, 383-384.
20 Calvin H. Johnson, "The Dubious Enumerated Powers Doctrine," *Constitutional Commentary*, no. 22 (2005): 35-37.
21 Ibid., 25.
22 Ibid., 38-39.
23 Ibid., 29-35.
24 Ray Raphael, *Constitutional Myths: What We Get Wrong and How to Get It Right* (New York: The New Press, 2013), 67.
25 Gordon Wood, *Empire of Liberty: A History of the Early Republic, 1789-1815* (New York: Oxford University Press, 2009), 71.
26 Ibid.
27 Klarman, *The Framers' Coup*, 367.
28 Ibid., 362.
29 Sean Illing, "The real reason we have an Electoral College: to protect slave states," *Vox*, November 12, 2016, https://www.vox.com/policy-and-politics/2016/11/12/13598316/donald-trump-electoral-college-slavery-akhil-reed-amar.
30 Klarman, *The Framers' Coup*, 200-203.
31 Adam Jentleson, *Kill Switch: The Rise of the Modern Senate and the Crippling of American Democracy* (New York: Liveright Publishing, 2021).
32 David Daley, *Rat F**cked: Why Your Vote Doesn't Count* (New York: Liveright Publishing, 2016).
33 Julia Kirschenbaum and Michael Li, "Gerrymandering Explained," *The Brennan Center*, August 12, 2021, https://www.brennancenter.org/our-work/research-reports/gerrymandering-explained.
34 Ari Berman, *Give Us the Ballot: The Modern Struggle for Voting Rights in America* (New York: Farrar, Straus and Giroux, 2015), 209-210, 220-221, 260, 262-263.
35 Priyanka Boghani, "How McConnell's Bid to Reshape the Federal Judiciary Extends Beyond the Supreme Court," *PBS*, October 16, 2020, https://www.pbs.org/wgbh/frontline/article/how-mcconnell-and-the-senate-helped-trump-set-records-in-appointing-judges/.
36 Aaron Rupar, "The Trump campaign's allegations of election fraud are a bunch of nonsense," *Vox*, November 6, 2020, https://www.vox.com/2020/11/6/21552720/trump-2020-campaign-election-irregularities-fraud.

37 Alex Emmons, "The Espionage Act Is Again Deployed Against a Government Official Leaking to the Media," *The Intercept*, October 9, 2019, https://theintercept.com/2019/10/09/the-espionage-act-is-again-deployed-against-a-government-official-leaking-to-the-media/.

38 Ben Shapiro, "Welcome to the Thugocracy," *Creators.com*, December 10, 2012, https://www.creators.com/read/ben-shapiro/12/12/welcome-to-the-thugocracy.

CHAPTER FOUR: CAPITALISM

1 Ha-Joon Chang, *Bad Samaritans: The Myth of Free Trade and the Secret History of Capitalism* (New York: Bloomsbury Publishing, 2008), 40-48.

2 Ibid., 48-56; Baptist, *The Half Has Never Been Told*.

3 Thomas Piketty, *A Brief History of Equality* (Cambridge: The Bellknap Press, 2022), 49-50.

4 Thomas Piketty, *Capital and Ideology* (Cambridge: The Bellknap Press, 2020), 374-375.

5 Noam Chomsky, *World Orders Old and New* (New York: Columbia University Press, 1996), 116-118.

6 Noam Chomsky, *Understanding Power* (New York: The New Press, 2002), 142.

7 Naomi Klein, *The Shock Doctrine: The Rise of Disaster Capitalism* (New York: Picador, 2007), 300-301; Judy Dempsey, "Study Looks at Mortality in Post-Soviet Era," *New York Times*, January 16, 2009, https://www.nytimes.com/2009/01/16/world/europe/16europe.html.

8 Vivek Chibber, *Locked in Place: State-Building and Late Industrialization in India* (Princeton: Princeton University Press, 2003).

9 Kevin Williamson, *The Politcally Incorrect Guide to Socialism* (Washington, DC: Regnery Publishing, 2011), 51-68.

10 Chibber, *Locked in Place*.

11 Chang, *Bad Samaritans*, 29.

12 Ibid., 26-28.

13 Ibid.

14 Mark Weisbrot, *Failed: What the "Experts" Got Wrong About the Global Economy* (Oxford: Oxford University Press, 2015), 58-59.

15 Ibid., 168-169.

16 See note 14 from Chapter One.

17 Paul Krugman, "A Money Too Far," *New York Times*, May 6, 2010, https://www.nytimes.com/2010/05/07/opinion/07krugman.html.

18 Maria A. Aris and Yi Wen, "Recovery from the Great Recession Has Varied around the World," *St. Louis Fed*, October 13, 2015, https://www.stlouisfed.org/

publications/regional-economist/october-2015/recovery-from-the-great-recession-has-varied-around-the-world.

19 Hickel, *The Divide*, 14-15.
20 Ibid., 50.
21 David Bacon, *The Right to Stay Home: How US Policy Drives Mexican Migration* (Boston: Beacon Press, 2013).
22 Matt Kibbe, "Matt Kibbe: Socialism Kills," YouTube, March 10, 2016, https://www.youtube.com/watch?v=9wg7jztTKew.
23 Richard Wilkinson and Kate Picket, *The Spirit Level: Why Greater Equality Makes Societies Stronger* (New York: Bloomsbury Press, 2009), 6-8; Reporters Without Borders, "2021 Press Freedom Index," *Reporters Without Borders*, 2021, https://rsf.org/en/ranking; Transparency International, "2020 Corruption Perceptions Index," *Transparency.org*, 2021, https://www.transparency.org/en/cpi/2020/index/nzl.
24 Matt Bruenig, "The Nordic Myths That Never Seem to Die," *People's Policy Project*, March 13, 2018, https://www.peoplespolicyproject.org/2018/03/13/the-nordic-myths-that-never-seem-to-die/; The Heritage Foundation, "2021 Index of Economic Freedom," *The Heritage Foundation*, 2021, https://www.heritage.org/index/ranking.
25 Mark Rank, Lawrence Eppard, and Heather Bullock, *Poorly Understood: What America Gets Wrong About Poverty* (Oxford: Oxford University Press, 2021), 73-81.
26 Tim Pat Coogan, *The Famine Plot: England's Role in Ireland's Greatest Tragedy* (New York: Palgrave Macmillan, 2012).
27 Mike Davis, *Late Victorian Holocausts: El Niño Famines and the Making of the Third World* (New York: Verso, 2001).
28 Adam Hochschild, *King Leopold's Ghost: A Story of Greed, Terror, and Heroism in Colonial Africa* (Boston: Houghton Mifflin Company, 1999).
29 Jean Drèze and Amartya Sen, *Hunger and Public Action* (Oxford: Clarendon Press, 1989), 204-225.
30 Matt Bruenig, "Bidencare System Will Kill 125,000 Through Uninsurance," *People's Policy Project*, July 15, 2019, https://www.peoplespolicyproject.org/2019/07/15/bidencare-system-will-kill-125000-through-uninsurance/.
31 Tirman, *The Deaths of Others*, 92, 168.
32 Brett Morris, "Agent Orange and unexploded bombs: America's 'human rights' record in Vietnam," *Vox*, June 2, 2016, https://www.vox.com/2016/6/2/11819304/vietnam-american-bombs.
33 Tirman, *The Deaths of Others*, 147-150.
34 Bevins, *The Jakarta Method*, 213.
35 Bevins, *The Jakarta Method*.
36 Drèze and Sen, *Hunger and Public Action*, 212.

37 Jonah Goldberg, *Liberal Fascism: The Secret History of the American Left from Mussolini to the Politics of Meaning* (New York: Doubleday, 2008), 7, Kindle.
38 Rand Paul, *The Case Against Socialism* (Northhampton: Broadside Books, 2019), 147-148, Kindle.
39 Goldberg, *Liberal Fascism*, 78-161.
40 Dinesh D'Souza, *The Big Lie: Exposing the Nazi Roots of the American Left* (Washington, DC: Regnery Publishing, 2017), 27, Kindle.
41 Paul, *The Case Against Socialism*, 139-141.
42 Robert Paxton, *The Anatomy of Fascism* (New York: Vintage Books, 2007), 64.
43 Ibid., 58-62.
44 Ibid., 49-50, 66.
45 Ibid., 60, 92-93.
46 Ibid., 63.
47 Ibid., 145, 151.
48 Esha Krishnaswamy, "The Economy of Evil," *Historic.ly* (blog), December 9, 2019, https://historicly.substack.com/p/the-economy-of-evil.
49 Paxton, *The Anatomy of Fascism*, 11.
50 Ibid., 136-137.
51 Rand Paul, *The Case Against Socialism*, 152-155.
52 Paxtion, *The Anatomy of Fascism*, 11, 145-146.
53 Goldberg, *Liberal Fascism*, 112-119.
54 Robert Goldstein, *Political Repression in Modern America: From 1870-1976* (Chicago: University of Illinios Press, 2001), 139-163.
55 David Schmitz, *Thank God They're on Our Side: The United States and Right-Wing Dictatorships, 1921-1965* (Chapel Hill: University of North Carolina Press, 1999); David Schmitz, *The U.S. and Right-Wing Dictatorships, 1965-1989* (Cambridge: Cambridge University Press, 2006).
56 Gillian Brockwell, "Wealthy bankers and businessmen plotted to overthrow FDR. A retired general foiled it," The Washington Post, January 13, 2001, https://www.washingtonpost.com/history/2021/01/13/fdr-roosevelt-coup-business-plot/.
57 Ludwig von Mises, *Liberalism: In the Classical Tradition* (San Francisco: Cobden Press, 1985), 51.
58 Paxton, *The Anatomy of Fascism*, 10-11.
59 Paul, *The Case Against Socialism*, 144.
60 Paxton, *The Anatomy of Fascism*, 146-147.
61 Jane Coaston, "Adolf Hitler was not a socialist," *Vox*, March 27, 2019, https://www.vox.com/2019/3/27/18283879/nazism-socialism-hitler-gop-brooks-gohmert.
62 Adolph Hitler, "On National Socialism and World Relations," (Speech delivered in the German Reichstag, January 30, 1937).
63 Paxton, *The Anatomy of Fascism*, 141.

64 Schmitz, *Thank God They're on Our Side*; Schmitz, *The U.S. and Right-Wing Dictatorships*.
65 John McMurtry, "How to Tell the Left From the Right," *Canadian Journal of Philosophy* IX, no. 3 (1979), 387-412.
66 Matt Bruenig, "Norway is Far More Socialist Than Venezuela," *People's Policy Project*, January 27, 2019, https://www.peoplespolicyproject.org/2019/01/27/norway-is-far-more-socialist-than-venezuela/.
67 Weisbrot, *Failed*, 229.
68 Associated Press, "What Socialism? Private sector still dominates Venezuelan economy despite Chavez crusade," *Fox News*, July 18, 2010, https://www.foxnews.com/world/what-socialism-private-sector-still-dominates-venezuelan-economy-despite-chavez-crusade.
69 Bruenig, "Norway is Far More Socialist Than Venezuela."
70 Mark Weisbrot and Jeffrey Sachs, *Economic Sanctions as Collective Punishment: The Case of Venezuela* (Center for Economic and Policy Research, April 2019).
71 Weisbrot, *Failed*, 210, 218-220.
72 Ibid., 167-233.
73 Marianna Mazzucato, *The Entrepreneurial State: Debunking Public vs. Private Myths in Risk and Innovation* (New York: Anthem Press, 2013).
74 Ibid., 104.
75 Rob Larson, *Bit Tyrants: The Political Economy of Silicon Valley* (Chicago: Haymarket Books, 2020), 75.

CHAPTER FIVE: ECONOMICS 101

1 Rank, Eppard, and Bullock, *Poorly Understood*, 23, 79, 151.
2 Chomsky, *Undocumented*, 117-151.
3 Rank, Eppard, and Bullock, *Poorly Understood*, 76, 79, 139, 151.
4 Ibid., 76.
5 Ibid., 15, 76.
6 Ibid., 74-75.
7 Ibid., 57-58.
8 Ibid., 60.
9 Ibid., 28-29.
10 Adrian Florido, "Black, Latino Two-Parent Families Have Half The Wealth Of White Single Parents," *NPR*, February 8, 2017, https://www.npr.org/sections/codeswitch/2017/02/08/514105689/black-latino-two-parent-families-have-half-the-wealth-of-white-single-parents.
11 Rank, Eppard, and Bullock, *Poorly Understood*, 55.

12 Ibid., 50.
13 See note 14 from Chapter One.
14 Rank, Eppard, and Bullock, *Poorly Understood*, 150-151.
15 Kat Chow, "'Model Minority' Myth Again Used As A Racial Wedge Between Asians And Blacks," *NPR*, April 19, 2017, https://www.npr.org/sections/codeswitch/2017/04/19/524571669/model-minority-myth-again-used-as-a-racial-wedge-between-asians-and-blacks.
16 Kenworthy, *Social Democratic America*, 35-36.
17 See note 14 from Chapter One.
18 Rank, Eppard, and Bullock, *Poorly Understood*, 131-133.
19 Kenworthy, *Social Democratic America*, 38-40.
20 Lane Kenworthy, "Is decoupling real?" *Lane Kenworthy* (blog), March 11, 2012, https://lanekenworthy.net/2012/03/11/is-decoupling-real/.
21 Kenworthy, *Social Democratic America*, 46-47.
22 Ibid., 36.
23 Ibid., 40.
24 Ibid., 42-46.
25 Ibid., 47-48.
26 See note 14 from Chapter One.
27 David Faris, *It's Time to Fight Dirty: How Democrats Can Build a Lasting Majority in American Politics* (Brooklyn: Melville House Publishing, 2018), 81-92.
28 Ross Barkan, "Defund the US Military and Rebuild the United States," *Jacobin*, October 10, 2020, https://jacobinmag.com/2020/10/defund-us-military-spending-trump-pentagon.
29 Chomsky, *Undocumented*, 1-151.
30 Faricy, *Welfare for the Wealthy*.
31 Baker, *Rigged*, 153-190.
32 Emmanuel Saez and Gabriel Zucman, *The Triumph of Injustice: How the Rich Dodge Taxes and How to Make Them Pay* (New York: W. W. Norton & Company, 2019), 14-15.
33 See note 14 from Chapter One.
34 Rank, Eppard, and Bullock, *Poorly Understood*, 120.
35 Ibid., 115.
36 Ibid., 68.
37 Rutger Bregman, *Utopia for Realists: How We Can Build the Ideal World* (New York: Little, Brown & Company, 2017), 29-47.
38 See note 14 from Chapter One.
39 Nicholas Eberstadt, *A Nation of Takers: America's Entitlement Epidemic* (West Conshohocken: Templeton Press, 2012), 4.
40 J. Bradford DeLong, "Shrugging Off Atlas," *Democracy Journal*, November 28,

2013. https://democracyjournal.org/magazine/28/shrugging-off-atlas/.
41. Matt Bruenig, "Cato Study Finds Medicare for All Saves $2 Trillion," *People's Policy Project*, July 30, 2018, https://www.peoplespolicyproject.org/2018/07/30/mercatus-study-finds-medicare-for-all-saves-2-trillion/.
42. Bruenig, "The Nordic Myths That Never Seem to Die."
43. Ibid.
44. Matt Bruenig, "Small populations make it harder to do what Nordic countries do," *Matt Bruenig* (blog), March 9, 2017, https://mattbruenig.medium.com/small-populations-make-it-harder-to-do-what-nordic-countries-do-c5a04715e657.
45. Steve Leisman, "Majority of Americans support progressive policies such as higher minimum wage, free college," *CNBC*, March 27, 2019, https://www.cnbc.com/2019/03/27/majority-of-americans-support-progressive-policies-such-as-paid-maternity-leave-free-college.html.
46. Jon Schwarz, "$10,000 Invested in Defense Stocks When Afghanistan War Began Worth Almost $100,000," *The Intercept*, August 16, 2021, https://theintercept.com/2021/08/16/afghanistan-war-defense-stocks/.
47. Mike Konczal, "The Voluntarism Fantasy," *Democracy Journal*, Spring 2014, https://democracyjournal.org/magazine/32/the-voluntarism-fantasy/.
48. Matt Bruenig, "How Much Money Would It Take to Eliminate Poverty in America?" *The Prospect*, September 24, 2013, https://prospect.org/power/much-money-take-eliminate-poverty-america/.
49. Tim Worstall, "America Has The World's Second Largest Social Welfare State," *Forbes*, October 8, 2015, https://www.forbes.com/sites/timworstall/2015/10/08/america-has-the-worlds-second-largest-social-welfare-state/.
50. Kenworthy, *Social Democratic America*, 75-81.
51. Saez and Zucman, *The Triumph of Injustice*, 135-138.

CHAPTER SIX: PERSONAL RESPONSIBILITY

1. David Horowitz, "Ten Reasons Why Reparations for Blacks is a Bad Idea for Blacks—and Racist Too" (Newspaper Advertisement, 2001).
2. Foner, *Reconstruction*, 105-106, 158-163, 171, 183-184.
3. Ibid., 200-202, 208, 421, 519, 593.
4. Ibid., 205.
5. Ibid., 68-69, 144-148, 164-165, 445-446, 454-455.
6. Andra Flynn, Susan Holmberg, Dorian Warren, and Felicia Wong, *The Hidden Rules of Race* (Cambridge: Cambridge University Press, 2017), 22-23.
7. Sugrue, *The Origins of the Urban Crisis*, 91-124.
8. Ibid., 48-51, 268; Richard Rothstein, *The Color of Law: A Forgotten History of How*

Our Government Segregated America (New York: Liveright Publishing, 2017), 53-54.
9. Flynn, Holmberg, Warren, and Wong, *The Hidden Rules of Race*, 71.
10. Sugrue, *The Origins of the Urban Crisis*, 44-46, 181-194.
11. Rothstein, *The Color of Law*, 64-65, 66, 74.
12. Sugrue, *The Origins of the Urban Crisis*, 194-197.
13. Ibid., 128, 140-141.
14. Ibid., 47-51
15. Ibid., 188-190, 197-203.
16. Flynn, Holmberg, Warren, and Wong, *The Hidden Rules of Race*, 81-82.
17. Sugrue, *The Origins of the Urban Crisis*, 91-92, 95-105.
18. Cowie, *Capital Moves*, 41-126.
19. Horowitz, "Ten Reasons Why Reparations for Blacks is a Bad Idea for Blacks—and Racist Too."
20. Joseph Crespino, *Strom Thurmond's America* (New York: Hill and Wang, 2012), 242.
21. Cohen, *Supreme Inequality*, 91-123.
22. P.R. Lockhart, "65 years after Brown v. Board of Education, school segregation is getting worse," *Vox*, May 10, 2019, https://www.vox.com/identities/2019/5/10/18566052/school-segregation-brown-board-education-report.
23. Flynn, Holmberg, Warren, and Wong, *The Hidden Rules of Race*, 73.
24. Rothstein, *The Color of Law*, 237.
25. Matthew Desmond, *Evicted: Poverty and Profit in the American City* (New York: Broadway Books, 2016), 44-46, 295-299.
26. Ibid., 303-305.
27. Keeanga-Yamahtta Taylor, *From #blacklivesmatter to Black Liberation* (Chicago: Haymarket Books, 2016), 75-106.
28. Ibid., 92-106.
29. Elizabeth Hinton, *From the War on Poverty to the War on Crime: The Making of Mass Incarceration in America* (Cambridge: Harvard University Press, 2016).
30. Taylor, *From #blacklivesmatter to Black Liberation*, 93-94; Kim Phillips-Fein, *Fear City: New York's Fiscal Crisis and the Rise of Austerity Politics* (New York: Metropolitan Books, 2017), 206-207; Flynn, Holmberg, and Wong, *The Hidden Rules of Race*, 91.
31. Rank, Eppard, and Bullock, *Poorly Understood*, 102-104.
32. See note 14 from Chapter One.
33. Michelle Alexander, *The New Jim Crow: Mass Incerceration in the Age of Colorblindness* (New York: The New Press, 2020), 148-151.
34. Ibid., 90-91.
35. Berman, *Give Us the Ballot*, 209-210, 220-221, 260, 262-263.

Notes

36 Cohen, *Supreme Inequality*, 135-166.
37 Ben Shapiro, "Say No to Campus Thuggery," (Speech, UC Berkeley, 2017); Ben Shapiro, "Tyrants in Training Who Promote Safe Spaces, Microaggressions and Attempt to Stifle Conservative Speech," (Young Americans for Freedom Lecture, Virginia Tech, April 1, 2016).
38 Flynn, Holmberg, Warren, and Wong, *The Hidden Rules of Race*, 50.
39 Alexander, *The New Jim Crow*, 87-89, 90-92, 104, 109-119, 133-137.

CHAPTER SEVEN: THE PARTY OF LINCOLN

1 Foner, *Reconstruction*, 575-582.
2 Heather Cox Richardson, *To Make Men Free: A History of the Republican Party* (New York: Basic Books, 2014), 94, 106-107.
3 Ibid., 109-138.
4 Ibid., 126-127.
5 Ibid., 130-131.
6 Ibid., 167.
7 Leonard Moore, *Citizen Klansmen: The Ku Klux Klan in Indiana, 1921-1928* (Chapel Hill: The University of North Carolina Press, 1991).
8 Richardson, *To Make Men Free*, 182-204.
9 Eric Schickler, *Racial Realignment: The Transformation of American Liberalism, 1932-1965* (Princeton: Princeton University Press, 2016), 186-187.
10 Ibid., 233.
11 Ian Haney López, *Dog Whistle Politics: How Coded Racial Appeals Have Reinvented Racism & Wrecked the Middle Class* (New York: Oxford University Press, 2014), 19.
12 Hinton, *From the War on Poverty to the War on Crime*.
13 Alexander, *The New Jim Crow*, 87-89, 90-92, 104, 109-119, 133-137.
14 Cohen, *Supreme Inequality*, 91-107.
15 Kirschenbaum and Li, "Gerrymandering Explained."
16 Berman, *Give Us the Ballot*, 273-314.
17 Richardson, *To Make Men Free*, 98-138, 171-192.
18 Schickler, *Racial Realignment*, 133.
19 See note 14 from Chapter One.
20 Schickler, *Racial Realignment*, 55-80.
21 Ibid., 105-118.
22 Ibid., 224-236.
23 Philip Bump, "When did black Americans start voting so heavily Democratic?" *The Washington Post*, July 7, 2015, https://www.washingtonpost.com/news/the-fix/wp/2015/07/07/when-did-black-americans-start-voting-so-heavily-democratic/.

24 Kevin D. Williamson, "The Party of Civil Rights," *National Review*, May 28, 2012, https://www.nationalreview.com/2012/05/party-civil-rights-kevin-d-williamson/.
25 Kevin Drum, "Why Did Democrats Lose the White South?" *Mother Jones*, November 25, 2015, https://www.motherjones.com/kevin-drum/2015/11/why-did-democrats-lose-white-south/.
26 Crespino, *Strom Thurmond's America*, 61-84.
27 Drum, "Why Did Democrats Lose the White South?"
28 López, *Dog Whistle Politics*, 16-17.
29 Earl Black and Merle Black, *The Rise of Southern Republicans* (Cambridge: The Bellknap Press, 2009), 209.
30 Ibid., 138-143, 152-153.
31 Joseph Lowndes, *From the New Deal to the New Right: Race and the Southern Origins of Modern Conservatism* (New Haven: Yale University Press, 2008), 116, 137.
32 Mark Levin, "Democrat 'Party Switch' Myth Debunked," YouTube, August 16, 2014, 3:34, https://www.youtube.com/watch?v=2RBFOTdY1yY.
33 Avdit Acharya, Matthew Blackwell, and Maya Sen, *Deep Roots: How Slavery Still Shapes Southern Politics* (Princeton: Princeton University Press, 2018), 49-75.
34 Ibid., 182-202.
35 Dinesh D'Souza, "D'Souza OBLITERATES leftist professor during Q&A session," YouTube, September 26, 2017, 5:22, https://www.youtube.com/watch?v=q3DQz5KBnpE.
36 Acharya, Blackwell, and Sen, *Deep Roots*, 96-100.
37 Williamson, "The Party of Civil Rights."
38 Dinesh D'Souza, "The myth of Nixon's Southern Strategy," *The Hill*, August 23, 2018, https://thehill.com/opinion/campaign/402754-the-myth-of-nixons-southern-strategy.
39 Schickler, *Racial Realignment*, 244-245, 252-270.
40 Lowndes, *From the New Deal to the New Right*, 56; Crespino, *Strom Thurmond's America*, 174.
41 Schickler, *Racial Realignment*, 258-259.
42 Crespino, *Strom Thurmond's America*, 129.
43 Ibid., 128.
44 Schickler, *Racial Realignment*, 261.
45 Crespino, *Strom Thurmond's America*, 134-135.
46 Schickler, *Racial Realignment*, 259-160.
47 Crespino, *Strom Thurmond's America*, 128.
48 Ibid., 111-112.
49 Ibid., 207-229.
50 Ibid., 225-226.
51 Lowndes, *From the New Deal to the New Right*, 137.

52 Ibid., 114-115.
53 Ibid., 122.
54 López, *Dog Whistle Politics*, 24.
55 Ibid.
56 Daniel Lucks, "Donald Trump, a true Reagan Republican," *Los Angeles Times*, July 19, 2020, https://www.latimes.com/opinion/story/2020-07-19/ronald-reagans-racism-cleared-the-way-for-trump.
57 López, *Dog Whistle Politics*, 58-59.
58 Ibid., 58.
59 Ibid., 105-106.
60 Ibid., 1.
61 Richardson, *To Make Men Free*, 107.
62 Schickler, *Racial Realignment*, 247.
63 Ibid.
64 Ibid.
65 Elizabeth McRae, *Mothers of Massive Resistance: White Women and the Politics of White Supremacy* (Oxford: Oxford University Press, 2018), 79.
66 Schickler, *Racial Realignment*, 249.
67 Ibid., 250.
68 Ibid., 244-245.
69 López, *Dog Whistle Politics*, 56-57.
70 Nancy MacLean, *Democracy in Chains: The Deep History of the Radical Right's Stealth Plan for America* (New York: Viking, 2017).
71 Martin Luther King, Jr., 'The Mississippi Challenge', in *The Autobiography of Martin Luther King, Jr.*, ed. Clayborne Carson (New York: Grand Central Publishing, 1998), 246.
72 Martin Luther King, Jr., "The quest for peace and justice," (Nobel Lecture, December 11, 1964).
73 Martin Luther King, Jr., "The Domestic Impact of the War," (National Labor Leadership Assembly for Peace, November, 1967).
74 Lowndes, *From the New Deal to the New Right*, 114-115.
75 Dan Amira, "The Eight Current Members of Congress Who Voted Against Martin Luther King Jr. Day," *New York Magazine*, January 21, 2013, https://nymag.com/intelligencer/2013/01/voted-against-mlk-day-mccain-hatch-grassley-shelby.html.
76 Thomas Jackson, *From Civil Rights to Human Rights: Martin Luther King, Jr., and the Struggle for Economic Justice* (Philadelphia: University of Pennsylvania Press, 2008), 42.
77 Ibid., 230.
78 Cohen, *Supreme Inequality*, 91-107.

79 See note 14 from Chapter One.
80 Berman, *Give Us the Ballot*, 209-210, 220-221, 260, 262-263.

CHAPTER EIGHT: THE PC THOUGHT POLICE

1 Edward Herman and Noam Chomsky, *Manufacturing Consent: The Political Economy of the Mass Media* (New York: Pantheon Books, 2002), 1-35.
2 Sam Raskin, "Nancy Pelosi to Leftist NYU Student: We're Capitalists, Deal With It," *NYU Local*, Febuary 1, 2017, https://nyulocal.com/nancy-pelosi-to-leftist-nyu-student-were-capitalists-deal-with-it-abf1e8e04e46; Joe Manchin, "Why I'm voting against the For the People Act," *Charleston Gazette Mail*, June 6, 2021, https://www.wvgazettemail.com/opinion/op_ed_commentaries/joe-manchin-why-im-voting-against-the-for-the-people-act/article_c7eb2551-a500-5f77-aa37-2e42d0af870f.html.
3 Herman and Chomsky, *Manufacturing Consent*, 14-18.
4 Ibid., 3-14.
5 Ibid., 26-28.
6 David Barsamian, "The Common Good: An Interview With Noam Chomsky," *The Sun Magazine*, November, 1997, https://www.thesunmagazine.org/issues/263/the-common-good.
7 Moskowitz, *The Case Against Free Speech: The First Amendment, Fascsism, and the Future of Dissent* (New York: Bold Type Books, 2019), 180-181.
8 Ibid., 154-156.
9 Ibid., 115.
10 Ibid., 135-141.
11 Ibid., 116-127.
12 Jeannine Mancini, "'I'm A Nobody And He Calls My Employer?' Elon Musk Silences Tesla Critics By Deactivating Twitter Accounts And Reaching Out To Their Employers," *Yahoo! Finance*, June 22, 2023, https://finance.yahoo.com/news/im-nobody-calls-employer-elon-130514911.html.
13 Moskowitz, *The Case Against Free Speech*.
14 Touré Reed, *Toward Freedom: The Case Against Race Reductionism* (New York: Verso, 2020).
15 Matthew McManus, *What is Post-Modern Conservatism: Essays on Our Hugely Tremendous Times* (Washington, USA: Zero Books, 2020) 123-124.
16 Ibid., 14-16.
17 Ibid.